CONTENTS GRADE 3

UNIT 1 SENTENCES

GRAMMAR SENTENCES

BUILD SKILLS

UNIT 2 NOUNS

GRAMMAR NOUNS

BUILD SKILLS

McGraw-Hill School Division

ii

UNIT 3 VERBS

● **GRAMMAR** VERBS

● **BUILD SKILLS**

McGraw-Hill School Division

UNIT 4 VERBS

GRAMMAR VERBS

BUILD SKILLS

UNIT 5 PRONOUNS

GRAMMAR PRONOUNS

BUILD SKILLS

UNIT 6 ADJECTIVES AND ADVERBS

McGraw-Hill School Division

Sentences

┌─ **RULES** ───┐

- A **sentence** is a group of words that tells a complete thought.

  This is a sentence: *We visit the pet store.*

- A **sentence fragment** is a group of words that does not tell a complete thought.

  This is not a sentence: *A small brown dog.*

- Every sentence begins with a capital letter.

└──┘

Circle each group of words that is a sentence.

1. Five fish swim in a tank.

2. Two tiny puppies.

3. The canaries chirp loudly.

4. The birds.

5. Three rabbits nibble on leaves.

6. A hamster sleeps in a cage.

7. One gerbil runs on a wheel.

8. Fluffy kittens.

9. A mouse hides in the straw.

10. Curls into a ball.

McGraw-Hill Language Arts
Grade 3, Unit 1, Sentences,
pages 2–3

At Home: Draw an animal you would find in a pet store.
Work with family members to write three complete
sentences about the animal.

1

Statements and Questions

> **RULES**
> - A **statement** is a sentence that tells something.
>   *The Stamp Museum has exhibits.*
> - A **question** is a sentence that asks something.
>   *What kinds of stamps can you see?*
> - Use a period to end a statement.
> - Use a question mark to end a question.

Tell whether the sentence is a statement or a question. Circle the correct word.

1. Stamp collecting is an interesting hobby.   statement   question

2. What country is this stamp from?   statement   question

3. Tani likes the smallest stamps.   statement   question

4. Some stamps are very colorful.   statement   question

5. Do you know how old this stamp is?   statement   question

6. How much can a rare stamp cost?   statement   question

7. Rare stamps can be very expensive.   statement   question

8. How many stamps does Tani have?   statement   question

9. What is the date on this stamp?   statement   question

10. The European stamp exhibit is my favorite.   statement   question

At Home: Ask family members to help you collect stamps that come in the mail. Write three statements about the stamps. Then rewrite the statements as questions.

McGraw-Hill Language Arts
Grade 3, Unit 1, Sentences,
pages 4–5   10

McGraw-Hill School Division

Commands and Exclamations

> **RULES**
> - A **command** is a sentence that tells or asks someone
>   to do something.
>   *Walk carefully in the cave.*
> - An **exclamation** is a sentence that shows strong feeling.
>   *Gee, this cave is huge!*

Is each sentence a command or an exclamation? Circle the correct word.

1. What a deep cave this is!   command   exclamation

2. Look at the walls.   command   exclamation

3. Don't leave the group.   command   exclamation

4. This cave is very dark!   command   exclamation

5. Wow, these rocks are shiny!   command   exclamation

6. Please walk slowly.   command   exclamation

7. Follow the tour guide.   command   exclamation

8. There are hundreds of bats!   command   exclamation

9. Don't frighten them.   command   exclamation

10. The bats sleep upside down!   command   exclamation

McGraw-Hill School Division

At Home: Choose an outdoor activity that you would like to do with your family. Write five commands about the activity. Then write the commands as exclamations.

Mechanics and Usage: Sentence Punctuation

┌─ **RULES** ───┐

• End a **statement** and a **command** with a **period.**

　Statement: *The Grand Canyon is made of layers of rock* | . |

　Command: *Look closely at the different layers* | . |

• End a **question** with a **question mark.**

　Question: *How many layers can you see* | ? |

• End an **exclamation** with an **exclamation mark.**

　Exclamation: *Wow, I can see hundreds of layers* | ! |

└──┘

Circle the correct end punctuation for each sentence.

1. Wow, this is beautiful   .   ?   !

2. Why is it called the Grand Canyon   .   ?   !

3. It is very big and deep   .   ?   !

4. Don't get too close to the edge   .   ?   !

5. How deep is it   .   ?   !

6. It is more than a mile deep   .   ?   !

7. What a great view this is   .   ?   !

8. Aren't you glad we came   .   ?   !

9. Take some pictures   .   ?   !

10. Where is my camera   .   ?   !

At Home: Find a picture you like of something in nature. Work with a family member to write all four kinds of sentences about the picture.

McGraw-Hill Language Arts
Grade 3, Unit 1, Sentences,
pages 8–9

4

10

McGraw-Hill School Division

Mixed Review

RULES

- A **sentence** expresses a complete thought. Every sentence begins with a capital letter. A **fragment** does not express a complete thought.
- A **statement** tells something. It ends with a **period.**
  We went sailing on Tuesday.
- A **question** asks something. It ends with a **question mark.**
  Did you have fun?
- A **command** tells or asks someone to do something. It ends with a **period.**
  Tell me what happened.
- An **exclamation** shows strong feeling. It ends with an **exclamation mark.**
  We had a really great day!

For each sentence below, write whether it is a **statement, question, command,** or **exclamation.** Then write the sentence using the correct end mark. Underline any fragments and make them complete sentences.

1. Max went to see the whales

_____

2. Where did he go

_____

3. The big boat

_____

4. Don't hang over the rail

_____

5. Wow, look at that whale

_____

McGraw-Hill School Division

At Home: Invite a family member to ask three questions about whales. Write the questions correctly. Find out the answers, then write them as statements.

Subjects in Sentences

RULES

- Every sentence has two parts. The **subject** of a sentence tells what or whom the sentence is about.

  Books can help us learn.

  subject → Books

- The subject of a sentence can be one word or more than one word.

  Many people enjoy reading.

  subject → Many people

Circle the subject in each sentence.

1. The library is a fun place to visit.

2. Hundreds of books sit on the shelves.

3. Adventure books are my favorite.

4. I like to curl up in a corner and read.

5. Some writers are very good at describing things.

6. They paint pictures with words.

7. Science fiction is fun to read, too.

8. Robots and spaceships are interesting.

9. Books about outer space make me want to become an astronaut.

10. I would like to visit another planet.

At Home: With a family member, write three sentences about a favorite story. Point out the subject in each sentence.

6

McGraw-Hill Language Arts
Grade 3, Unit 1, Sentences,
pages 12–13

10

McGraw-Hill School Division

Predicates in Sentences

┌─ **RULES** ═══
│ • Every sentence has two parts. The **predicate** of a sentence tells
│   what the subject does or is.
│
│   *The children* **explored the old fort.**
│
│   predicate → | explored the old fort. |
│
│   *The fort* **had huge doors.**
│
│   predicate → | had huge doors. |
└──

Circle the predicate in each sentence.

1. The guide showed the children the fort.

2. The walls are stacked logs.

3. Some of the logs are missing.

4. A high tower stands at that corner.

5. A watchman sat in the tower.

6. He watched for signs of trouble.

7. A small town grew up around the fort.

8. Families of soldiers lived in the fort.

9. The children saw the old schoolroom.

10. The guide took a picture of them.

At Home: Look in a favorite book to find a paragraph about exploring. Share it with a family member. Point out four predicates.

Combining Sentences: Compound Sentences

RULES

- Two related **sentences can be combined** with a comma and the word *and*.
- A **compound sentence** is a sentence that contains two sentences joined by *and*.

Maria has a pet rabbit.   *It likes to eat lettuce.*

Maria has a pet rabbit **,** **and** *it likes to eat lettuce.*

Use the word in ( ) to join each pair of sentences.

1. Rabbits are cute. (and) They are also very shy animals.

_____

_____

2. They have large ears. (and) They have a good sense of smell.

_____

_____

3. Rabbits feed in the evening. (and) They are always alert.

_____

_____

4. Rabbits make nice pets. (and) They need lots of care.

_____

_____

5. Rabbits eat a lot. (and) They grow fast.

_____

_____

At Home: Ask family members to listen as you combine two related sentences about an animal. Use the word *and*.

McGraw-Hill School Division

Mechanics and Usage:
Correcting Run-on Sentences

┌─ **RULES** ─────────────────────────────────┐

• A **run-on sentence** joins together two or more sentences.

The clowns rode on the elephants they waved to the crowd.

• Correct a run-on sentence by separating two ideas into two sentences.

The clowns rode on the elephants. They waved to the crowd.

• Correct a run-on sentence by writing it as a compound sentence.

*The clowns rode on the elephants, **and** they waved to the crowd.*

└──┘

Draw a line between the two sentences. The first one is done for you.

1. The circus has jugglers and tumblers/it has wild animals, too.

2. The circus has horseback riders they perform tricks.

3. Riders leap on and off a moving horse they leap through hoops.

4. Clowns are important in the circus they make people laugh.

5. A traveling circus has a parade it has wagons and bands.

6. People line the streets to see the parade the circus performers wave.

7. Bands play marching music clowns do funny tricks.

8. The circus is held in a tent it has room for many people.

9. People of all ages go to the circus they have fun.

10. The circus stays for two weeks it will be back next year.

McGraw-Hill Language Arts
Grade 3, Unit 1, Sentences,
10 **pages 18–19**

At Home: Tell someone in your family what you know about the circus. Use compound sentences.

9

Mixed Review

> **RULES**
> * The **subject** of a sentence tells whom or what the sentence is about.
> * The **predicate** of a sentence tells what the subject does or is.
>
>   subject   predicate
>   ↓   ↓
>   *My family*   *likes to visit the zoo.*
>
> * A **compound sentence** contains two related sentences joined by the word *and*.
> * A **run-on sentence** contains two or more sentences that should stand alone.

A. Read each sentence. Circle the subject and underline the predicate.

1. Tigers have stripes.

2. The stripes help the tigers hide.

3. Tigers belong to the cat family.

4. White tigers are very rare.

5. Other big cats include lions and panthers.

B. Read each sentence. Next to each one, write **compound** or **run-on.**

6. Some people see tigers at the zoo, and other people see tigers at the circus. _____

7. I took photos of the tigers, and Jack sketched the lions. _____

8. A trainer can teach a tiger to jump through a hoop sometimes the hoop is on fire. _____

9. The roar of a tiger is very loud it is scary. _____

10. Lions roar loudly in the jungle, and the other animals run away. _____

At Home: With a family member, write sentences about other animals in the cat family. Circle the subjects and underline the predicates.

McGraw-Hill Language Arts
Grade 3, Unit 1, Sentences,
pages 20–21
10

McGraw-Hill School Division

Common Errors with Fragments and Run-on Sentences

> **RULES**
> - A **sentence fragment** does <u>not</u> express a complete thought.
>   This is a sentence fragment: *Was howling.*
> - You can often correct a sentence fragment by adding a subject or a predicate.
> - A **run-on sentence** contains two or more sentences that should stand alone.
>   This is a run-on sentence: *It is raining we are getting wet.*
> - You can correct a run-on sentence by writing it as **two sentences,** or as a **compound sentence.**
>   Here are two separate sentences: *It is raining. We are getting wet.*
>   Here is a compound sentence: *It is raining, and we are getting wet.*

Write **sentence, fragment,** or **run-on sentence** after each group of words.

1. The weather forecaster. _____

2. There is a storm approaching the coast. _____

3. A bad one. _____

4. Should get. _____

5. Stay tuned to this station for updates. _____

6. The next day was sunny and clear trees and other debris covered the ground. _____

7. A group of volunteers came by to help us clean up the Coast Guard went up and down the coast. _____

8. Was very lucky. _____

9. Now our neighborhood is clean again. _____

10. We have a new club we talk about ways to keep our neighborhood safe during a storm. _____

10 **McGraw-Hill Language Arts**
Grade 3, Unit 1, Sentences,
pages 22–23

At Home: Get a copy of your favorite book. Read a paragraph aloud to a family member. Point out the subject and predicate in at least four sentences.

11

Study Skills: Dictionary

> **RULES**
>
> You use a **dictionary** to find the meanings of words. A dictionary also shows you how words are spelled.
>
> - **Guide words** show the first and last words on a page. They help you locate the entry word.
> - **Entry words** are all the words explained in a dictionary. They are listed in ABC order.

Number the words in each list to show the correct ABC order.

1. hut _____
   guide _____
   icicle _____

2. track _____
   skunk _____
   skate _____

3. junk _____
   jade _____
   jellyfish _____

4. rough _____
   rung _____
   ranch _____

Read each pair of guide words. Circle the word that you would find on a dictionary page with those guide words.

5. march/mattress   margin   next   nose
6. float/flute   table   flood   three
7. cement/cinder   earth   echo   center
8. salt/sap   zero   sample   zoo
9. anger/apple   comb   appeal   cook
10. pin/pioneer   pink   gate   gear

At Home: Ask a family member to list three words. You put them in ABC order. Have the family member check to make sure you are correct.

12

McGraw-Hill Language Arts
Grade 3, Unit 1, Study Skills,
pages 30–31

10

McGraw-Hill School Division

Vocabulary: Time-Order Words

- A time-order word or phrase tells when things happen and in what order.

  Before *we left on our fishing trip, we ate cereal.*

  Next, *we packed a picnic lunch.*

first	second	afterward
next	finally	before
then	third	a long time

Read each sentence. Write on the line the word or words that show time-order.

1. Fishing can be fun, but first you have to know what to do.

   _____

2. You need a good fishing rod before anything else.

   _____

3. After you get the rod, practice casting at home in the yard.

   _____

4. While you are practicing, ask a friend to dig up some worms.

   _____

5. Next, learn how to put the worm on the hook.

   _____

6. You are now ready to try to catch a fish!

   _____

7. You might have to sit a long time without getting a bite.

   _____

8. A fish might not immediately grab the worm.

   _____

9. A fish may tug on the worm to tease you first.

   _____

10. Finally, the fish will grab the worm, and you will catch it!

    _____

McGraw-Hill Language Arts
Grade 3, Unit 1, Vocabulary,
pages 32–33

At Home: Write directions for making a peanut butter sandwich.
Use time-order words like *first, second, next,* and *finally.* Ask a
family member to follow your directions.

10   13

Composition: Main Idea and Supporting Details

- The **main idea** tells what a piece of writing is all about.
- In a good **paragraph,** all sentences should work together to tell about one main idea.
- The main idea of a paragraph is usually told in a **topic sentence.**
- **Supporting details** help to develop and support the main idea.
- If a detail has nothing important to say about the main idea, take it out.
- You can use **time-order words** such as *first, next,* and *before* to connect your ideas.

Read each group of sentences. Find the sentence that tells the main idea and underline it.

1. First, my father spread a blanket on the grass. Then we ate chicken and salad. We spent Saturday afternoon at a family picnic.

2. My sister and I jumped right in. We swam to the raft. We had fun swimming in the lake.

3. My cousins played softball in the field nearby. Marcus hit a home run! Ruthie is the best pitcher.

4. My mother and aunt brought sandwiches. There was so much wonderful food. There was a basket of apples and pears.

5. We flew kites. We played tag. Everyone enjoyed our day in the park.

14

At Home: Find a newspaper article and share it with a family member. Point out the main idea and two supporting details in the article.

McGraw-Hill Language Arts
Grade 3, Unit 1, Composition,
pages 34–35 | 5 |

McGraw-Hill School Division

Nouns

┌─ **RULES** ─────────────────────────────────────┐

• A **noun** is a word that names a person, place, or thing.

    a person → *boy, woman, worker*

    a place → *pool, field, yard*

    a thing → *milk, ball, stone*

    The **beekeeper** lives nearby. → *Beekeeper* is a **person.**

    He works in his **yard.** → *Yard* is a **place.**

    He gathers **honey.** → *Honey* is a **thing.**

  The words **beekeeper, yard,** and **honey** are all nouns.

└───┘

Circle the noun in each sentence.

1. There are many hives here.

2. Bees fly all around.

3. They collect pollen.

4. They won't sting the beekeeper.

5. He wears special clothes.

6. He shows us a honeycomb.

7. It is made of wax.

8. There are cells in it.

9. This is how they make honey.

10. We keep it in jars.

10

McGraw-Hill Language Arts
Grade 3, Unit 2, Nouns,
pages 78–79

At Home: With a family member, brainstorm nouns about bees. Draw some cells like a honeycomb in which to write your nouns.

15

Singular and Plural Nouns

┌─ **RULES** ───

- A **singular noun** names one person, place, or thing.

    person, place, or thing → *boy, school, book*

- A **plural noun** names more than one person, place, or thing.

    persons, places, or things → *boys, schools, books*

- Add **-s** to form the plural of most singular nouns.

    cat + **s** = *cats*   *girl* + **s** = *girls*

- Add **-es** to form the plural of nouns that end in **s, sh, ch,** or **x.**

    inch + **es** = *inches*   *brush* + **es** = *brushes*

    dress + **es** = *dresses*   *fox* + **es** = *foxes*

└──

Read each item on the School Fix-It List. Decide if the underlined noun is singular or plural. Write **singular** or **plural** on the line.

School Fix-It List

1. Check tires on school <u>bus</u>. _____
2. Trim <u>bushes</u> near door. _____
3. Paint bike <u>rack</u>. _____
4. Replace glass in gym <u>windows</u>. _____
5. Check <u>light</u> in hallway. _____
6. Rake <u>leaves</u> on playground. _____
7. Paint front <u>office</u>. _____
8. Put empty <u>boxes</u> in trash bin. _____
9. Repair school <u>clock</u>. _____
10. Get new <u>cups</u> for office. _____

At Home: With a family member, make a Fix-It List of your own. Tell about toys, sports equipment, clothes, or pets that you need to take care of. Use singular and plural nouns.

16

McGraw-Hill Language Arts
Grade 3, Unit 2, Nouns,
pages 80–81 /10

McGraw-Hill School Division

Plural Nouns with *-ies*

RULES
- If a noun ends in a consonant and the letter **y,** change the **y** to **i** and add **-es** to form the **plural.**

  cherry → cherr**ies**

  I tasted one **cherry.** ← singular

  She tasted three **cherries.** ← plural

Write the plural form of each noun in the list.

1. country

_____

2. guppy

_____

3. ferry

_____

4. daisy

_____

5. grocery

_____

6. secretary

_____

7. baby

_____

8. story

_____

9. puppy

_____

10. family

_____

McGraw-Hill Language Arts
Grade 3, Unit 2, Nouns,
pages 82–83

At Home: Draw a picture of a farm, showing ponies, bunnies, and puppies. Label the animals. Show your picture to a family member. Tell how to spell the plural forms.

10

17

More Plural Nouns

RULES

- Some nouns have special plural forms.

Singular	**Plural**
One ma**n**	Two m**en**
One woma**n**	Three wom**en**
One t**oo**th	Four t**ee**th
One m**ou**se	Five m**ice**
One child	Six child**ren**

- A few nouns have the same singular and plural forms.

Singular	**Plural**
One sheep	Two sheep
One deer	Three deer
One moose	Four moose
One fish	Five fish
One trout	Six trout

Write the plural form for each noun.

1. child _____   6. man _____

2. tooth _____   7. fish _____

3. deer _____   8. mouse _____

4. moose _____   9. trout _____

5. sheep _____   10. woman _____

At Home: Look for a book in the library about sheep, deer, geese, or moose. Share it with a family member. Share what you have learned about singular and plural nouns.

McGraw-Hill Language Arts
Grade 3, Unit 2, Nouns,
pages 84–85

McGraw-Hill School Division

10

Common and Proper Nouns

> **RULES**
>
> There are two kinds of nouns, common nouns and proper nouns.
>
> • A **common noun** names **any** person, place, or thing. It begins with a small letter.
>
> • A **proper noun** names a **special** person, place, or thing. It can have more than one word. Each important word in a proper noun begins with a capital letter.
>
> | | |
> |---|---|
> | *a friend* | *Heather Martin* |
> | *a city* | *Los Angeles* |
> | *a day* | *Thursday* |
> | *a river* | *the Mississippi River* |

Underline each common noun.
Circle each proper noun.

1. Lindhurst

2. Friday

3. Lake Shore Drive

4. river

5. building

6. doctor

7. Mary Lee

8. Rocky Mountains

9. New Jersey

10. park

At Home: Look at a book of maps with a member of your family. Find names of cities, countries, and bodies of water. Tell why these names begin with capital letters.

Mechanics and Usage: Capitalization

RULES
- **Capitalize** each important word of a **proper noun.**
- The name of a **day, month,** or **holiday** begins with a capital letter.
    Tuesday   July   President's Day
- Words in titles of books begin with capital letters.
    Nate's Treasure   Ali Baba and the Forty Thieves
- Do not capitalize a word like *of*, *the*, and *in* unless it is the first word of a book title.

Read each sentence. Write the underlined proper noun correctly.

1. Geraldo got a new book on <u>monday</u>.

   _____

2. The title of the book is <u>nate the great</u>.

   _____

3. He will try to finish his book before <u>thanksgiving</u>.

   _____

4. Ravi wants to read <u>eyes of the dragon</u>.

   _____

5. It is about a dragon painter named <u>ch'en jung</u>.

   _____

6. He will get it at the library on <u>saturday</u>. _____

7. The library closes for two weeks in <u>december</u>. _____

8. We are joining a book club in <u>january</u>. _____

9. The meetings are on <u>wednesday</u> afternoons. _____

10. There is no school on <u>new year's day</u>. _____

At Home: Ask a family member to name the month in which they were born, a favorite holiday, and favorite book. Write each proper noun correctly.

20

McGraw-Hill Language Arts
Grade 3, Unit 2, Nouns,
pages 88–89

10

McGraw-Hill School Division

Mixed Review

┌─ **RULES** ───┐

• A **singular noun** names one person, place, or thing.

• A **plural noun** names more than one person, place, or thing.

  Add **-s** to form most plural nouns: *desk → desks*

  Add **-es** to form the plural of nouns
  that end in *s, sh, ch,* or *x:*   *lunch → lunches*

  Some nouns have special plural
  forms: *mouse → mice*

• A **common noun** names any person, place, or thing.

• A **proper noun** names a special person, place, or thing and
  begins with a capital letter.

  Common nouns: *city, holiday, state*

  Proper nouns: *Chicago, Thanksgiving, Utah*

└──┘

Read each sentence. Decide if the underlined noun is singular or
plural. Then write **singular** or **plural** under it.

1. We had a picnic at the <u>beach</u>.

_____

2. The <u>sun</u> was shining brightly.

_____

3. Anya brought the <u>sandwiches</u>.

_____

4. Did anyone remember to bring <u>dishes</u>?

_____

5. We ran to put our <u>feet</u> in the water.

_____

At Home: Look at a magazine or newspaper with a family
member. Identify common or proper nouns. Are they
singular or plural? See how many you can find.

Singular Possessive Nouns

RULES

- A **possessive noun** shows ownership. It tells who or what owns or has something.
- To form a singular possessive noun, add **'s** to the singular noun.

singular noun + **'s** = singular possessive noun

boy + 's = boy's   horse + 's = horse's

the boy's coat   the horse's stall

Write the possessive noun in each sentence.

1. The art show's theme is "Color in Nature." _____

2. Anna's picture shows a winter scene. _____

3. A polar bear's fur blends with the snow. _____

4. Emma's drawing is in the art show, too. _____

5. A mouse's dark fur blends with dirt and rocks. _____
6. The grasshopper's color blends into the grass.

_____

7. Robert's picture has a jungle setting. _____
8. The leopard's spots make the animal hard to see.

_____

9. The tiger's stripes blend into the shadows. _____
10. Nature's paintbox helps many creatures stay safe.

_____

At Home: Find something in your home that belongs to a family member. Make a sign for it, using a possessive noun.

22

McGraw-Hill Language Arts
Grade 3, Unit 2, Nouns,
pages 92–93

10

McGraw-Hill School Division

Plural Possessive Nouns

> **RULES**
> - Add an apostrophe (') to make most plural nouns possessive.
>   *The birds' feathers are beautiful.*
> - Add an apostrophe (') and an **-s** to form the possessive of plural nouns that do not end in **-s.**
>   *The children's books are on the shelf.*

Write **singular** or **plural** for each underlined possessive noun.

1. the <u>children's</u> faces

_____

2. the <u>elephants'</u> ears

_____

3. the <u>monkeys'</u> tails

_____

4. the <u>bee's</u> sting

_____

5. the <u>zookeeper's</u> hands

_____

6. the <u>turtles'</u> tank

_____

7. the <u>zebra's</u> stripes

_____

8. the <u>men's</u> cameras

_____

9. the <u>cage's</u> door

_____

10. the <u>leopard's</u> spots

_____

McGraw-Hill Language Arts
Grade 3, Unit 2, Nouns,
pages 94–95
10

At Home: With a family member, think of people you know who have pets. Write a list of the pets, using possessive nouns; for instance, *Tanya's kitten.*

23

Combining Sentences: Nouns

> ## RULES
> - You can combine two sentences by joining two nouns.
> - **Combining sentences** can make your writing more interesting.
> - Use the word **and** to combine the two nouns. Leave out the words that repeat.
>
> *Luis* | *built a birdhouse.*
>
> ↓
>
> *Kenji* | *built a birdhouse.*
>
> ↓
>
> *Luis* **and** *Kenji* | *built a birdhouse.*

Read each pair of sentences. Circle the parts that are alike. Then use **and** to combine the sentences.

1. Dean studied birds.
   Jan studied birds.

   _____

2. They saw a mother robin.
   They saw a father robin.

   _____

3. The robins got straw.
   The robins got moss.

   _____

4. The nest was soft.
   The nest was warm.

   _____

5. Insects are what robins eat.
   Worms are what robins eat.

   _____

At Home: Write a sentence about what a pet can do. Ask a family member to think of another sentence about that pet. Combine the sentences using *and*.

24

**McGraw-Hill Language Arts
Grade 3, Unit 2, Nouns,
pages 96–97**

5

McGraw-Hill School Division

Mechanics and Usage: Abbreviations

> ┌─ **RULES** ─────────────────────────────
> - An **abbreviation** is a shortened form of a word.
>   *Doctor Santos = Dr. Santos*
> - An abbreviation begins with a capital letter and ends with a period.
> - You can abbreviate titles before a name.
>   *Mrs. Santos   Dr. McCabe   Ms. Gould*
> - You can abbreviate days of the week.
>   *Sun. Mon. Tues. Wed. Thurs. Fri. Sat.*
> - You can abbreviate some months.
>   *Jan. Feb. Mar. Apr. Aug. Sept. Oct. Nov. Dec.*

Write whether each underlined abbreviation is a **title,** a **day** of the week, or a **month** of the year.

1. until <u>Sat.</u> _____

2. <u>Dr.</u> Cook's friend _____

3. by <u>Mon.</u> _____

4. beginning of <u>Dec.</u> _____

5. early <u>Aug.</u> _____

6. with <u>Mr.</u> Reynolds _____

7. next <u>Feb.</u> _____

8. every <u>Thurs.</u> _____

9. <u>Mrs.</u> Riley's class _____

10. appointment on <u>Wed.</u> _____

McGraw-Hill Language Arts
Grade 3, Unit 2, Nouns,
pages 98–99

At Home: With your family, make a map of your neighborhood. List adults and children in each home. Use abbreviations for titles of people.

25

McGraw-Hill School Division

Mixed Review

RULES

- A **possessive noun** shows who or what owns something.
- Add an apostrophe (') and an **-s** to a singular noun to make it possessive.

  My | **sister's** | class went to the zoo.

- Add an apostrophe to make most plural nouns possessive.

  The | **animals'** | keepers brought them food.

- Add an apostrophe and an **-s** to form the possessive of plural nouns that do not end in **-s.**

  The | **children's** | favorite place was the snake house.

Write the possessive noun from each sentence.

1. The zookeeper's office is by the main entrance. _____

2. The monkeys' house is near the elephant pen. _____

3. The elephants' keeper is feeding them. _____

4. The giraffe's baby is standing near her mother. _____

5. The man's camera is ready. _____

6. The camera's flash is bright. _____

7. The baby's picture will be in the paper. _____

8. The picture's quality will be clear. _____

9. The children's teacher pointed to the monkeys. _____

10. The animals' antics made them laugh. _____

At Home: Make a list of things you can see at the zoo. With a family member, write five sentences that use possessive nouns. For example, *The monkeys' tails are long.*

26

McGraw-Hill Language Arts
Grade 3, Unit 2, Nouns,
pages 100–101

/10

McGraw-Hill School Division

Common Errors with Plurals and Possessives

RULES

Writers often make mistakes when writing plural nouns and possessive nouns.

- A **plural noun** names more than one person, place, or thing.

  farmers   fields   geese

- A **possessive noun** shows who or what owns or has something.

- To form the possessive of a singular noun, add an **'s**.

  The **farmer's** *field is filled with wheat.*

- To form the possessive of a plural noun that ends in *-s,* add an apostrophe (').

  The **farmers'** *fields are filled with wheat.*

- To form the possessive of a plural noun that does not end in *-s,* add an **'s**.

  The **geese's** *eggs are large.*

Read the sentences. Circle the word in ( ) that is the correct plural or possessive noun. Then write it on the line.

1. The (children's, childrens', childrens) teacher took them to a farm.

_____

2. The (farmers', farmer's, farmers) tractor is red.

_____

3. The (geese, gooses', goose's) feathers are soft.

_____

4. The (geese, goose, goose's) live in a big pen.

_____

5. The (pigs, pigs', pig's) name is Wilbur.

_____

McGraw-Hill School Division

McGraw-Hill Language Arts
Grade 3, Unit 2, Nouns,
pages 102–103

5

At Home: With a family member, think of four animals you might find on a farm. Then write sentences about the animals using plural and possessive nouns.

27

Study Skills: Library Resources

- The **library** is a good source of information. To locate information in the library, use the **Library Card Catalog** or **PAC (Public Access Catalog).** In most libraries, the catalog, or PAC, is on the computer.
- The **card catalog** lists all the books and materials in the library. The card catalog contains a **title card** and an **author card** for every book. Each nonfiction book also has a **subject card.** The cards are arranged in alphabetical order.
- Every book has a **call number** that identifies what category of book it is. It can help you find the book on the shelf.

Title Cards	**Author Cards**	**Subject Cards**
↓	↓	↓
If you know the **title** of the book you want, use this card.	If you know the **author** of the book you want, use this card.	If you know the **subject** of the book you want, use this card.

Write what kind of card in the card catalog you would use to find the following information.

1. Books about kangaroos _____

2. A story about a pretend place by Alice McLerran _____

3. A list of books by Beverly Cleary _____

4. A book called *Ibis: A True Whale Story* _____

5. Books about George Washington _____

6. A mystery story by Johnny Alcorn _____

7. A book called *The Puffins Are Back* _____

8. A book about a cowboy named Pecos Bill _____

9. A list of books by Gail Gibbons _____

10. Books about football _____

At Home: With a family member, choose a subject, author, or title of a book. Then go to the library together and look for the book by using the card catalog.

28

McGraw-Hill Language Arts
Grade 3, Unit 2, Study Skills,
pages 110–111
10

Vocabulary: Compound Words

A **compound word** is a word made by joining two or more words together.

mail + box	A **mailbox** is a **box for mail.**
paint + brush	A **paintbrush** is a **brush for painting.**
sun + light	**Sunlight** is **light from the sun.**
back + pack	A **backpack** is a **pack you wear on your back.**

Circle the compound word in each pair. Write the two words that make up the compound word on the lines below it.

1. basketball, berries

_____ _____

2. moonlight, mostly

_____ _____

3. notice, notebook

_____ _____

4. surely, sunburn

_____ _____

5. halfway, habit

_____ _____

6. haircut, handle

_____ _____

7. topic, toothache

_____ _____

8. seat, seashore

_____ _____

9. windowsill, windy

_____ _____

10. barefoot, baby

_____ _____

McGraw-Hill Language Arts
Grade 3, Unit 2, Vocabulary,
pages 112–113

10

At Home: Find items in your home with compound word names, such as *toothbrush, washcloth,* and *bathtub.* Make a list of these words and explain it to a family member.

Composition: Organization

- Writing about ideas, events, or instructions is like solving a problem. You must present the details in an order that makes sense.

- What are you going to tell about? Begin with a **topic sentence** that tells the main idea.

- What order should you choose? Try to tell things in time order with **step-by-step details**. Keep in mind what is **first, second, third**, and so on.

- How can special words help? Begin your sentences with words such as *First, Next,* and *Last.*

Rewrite the paragraph on the lines below. Draw a line under the topic sentence. Circle each time-order word.

    Follow these easy steps to give your dog a bath. First, put your dog in a tub of warm water. Second, wash your dog all over using baby shampoo. Next, rinse your dog with clean water. Last, dry your dog with thick, dry towels.

_____

_____

_____

_____

_____

_____

_____

_____

_____

At Home: With a family member, make a chart about washing dishes. Tell what to do in 4 or 5 steps. Make sure the steps are in order. Then post your chart on the refrigerator.

McGraw-Hill Language Arts
Grade 3, Unit 2, Composition,
pages 114–115

5

McGraw-Hill School Division

Action Verbs

Read each sentence. Ask what the subject does. Find the words that show action. Circle each action verb.

1. Mike goes to his art class.

2. The students button their smocks.

3. The students mold the clay.

4. Mike creates a clay pot.

5. The teacher takes the pot to the kiln.

6. Artists work with different materials.

7. Potters use clay, a potter's wheel, and a kiln.

8. A potter's wheel turns very quickly.

9. The artists make pottery of many shapes and sizes.

10. Later, everyone paints the pottery.

McGraw-Hill Language Arts
Grade 3, Unit 3, Verbs,
pages 160–161

At Home: Use action words to tell your family what you did at school today.

McGraw-Hill School Division

Present-Tense Verbs

RULES

- The **tense** of a verb tells when the action takes place.
- Verbs in the **present tense** tell what happens now.
- Follow these rules when you use present-tense verbs with singular subjects.
- Add **-s** to most singular verbs in → *Miss Muffet sits down.* the present tense.
- Add **-es** to verbs that end in *sh,* → *The spider watches Miss Muffet.* *ch, ss, s, zz,* or *x.*
- Change **y** to **i** and add **-es** to → *Miss Muffet cries for help.* verbs that end in a consonant and a **y** together.

Circle the verb in ( ) that has the correct spelling.

1. The gingerbread man (runes, runs) away.

2. The fox (carrys, carries) him through the water.

3. Everyone (chases, chasies) after him.

4. Mama Bear (fixes, fixs) porridge.

5. Goldilocks (gets, getes) lost in the woods.

6. Baby Bear (watchs, watches) the girl sleep.

7. Gepetto (wishs, wishes) on a star.

8. Pinocchio (trys, tries) to be an actor.

9. Gepetto (misses, misss) Pinocchio.

10. Pinocchio (changes, changies) into a donkey.

McGraw-Hill School Division

At Home: Draw pictures of a favorite storybook character doing something. Tell a family member about the character, using present-tense verbs.

32

McGraw-Hill Language Arts Grade 3, Unit 3, Verbs, pages 162–163

/10

Subject-Verb Agreement

RULES
- A **present-tense** verb must agree with its subject.
- Do not add **-s** or **-es** to a present-tense verb when the subject is plural.
  The children need a computer.
  Computers change our lives.
- Do not add **-s** or **-es** to a present-tense verb when the subject is *I* or *you*.
  You use computers for schoolwork.
  I see computers every day.

Write the correct form of the verb in ( ).

1. Computers (give, gives) us information.

_____

2. The information (help, helps) us.

_____

3. We (know, knows) some things.

_____

4. A student (learn, learns) many new things.

_____

5. You (find, finds) interesting facts.

_____

6. Many people (buy, buys) computers.

_____

7. A teacher (load, loads) software into the computer.

_____

8. I (put, puts) in the disks.

_____

9. You (press, presses) the keys.

_____

10. The keys (give, gives) commands.

_____

McGraw-Hill Language Arts
Grade 3, Unit 3, Verbs,
pages 164–165
10

At Home: Tell your family how you use or would like to use computers in school. Make sure that you use correct subject-verb agreement.

33

Mechanics and Usage: Letter Punctuation

┌─ **RULES** ───
│ • Use a capital letter for the first word and the name in the greeting
│   and the closing of a letter.
│   *Dear Uncle Peter,*
│   *Love,*
│   *Pat*
│ • Put a comma at the end of the greeting. Put a comma between
│   the closing and the signature.
│   *Dear Uncle Peter,*
│   *Love,*
│   *Pat*
└───

Circle the correct answer in each pair.

1. Dear, Chris   Dear Chris,

2. Sincerely,   Sincerely
    Clarissa   Clarissa

3. Yours truly,   Yours Truly,
    Kevin   Kevin

4. Dear Mario,   dear Mario,

5. Your Friend   Your friend,
    Yuko   Yuko

6. Dear grandpa,   Dear Grandpa,

7. Love   Love,
    Courtney   Courtney

8. dear Sonia,   Dear Sonia,

9. Sincerely yours,   Sincerely Yours,
    Stephen   Stephen

10. Dear Jada,   Dear Jada

Jan. 1, 2004

Dear Gina,
    I had fun. Hope you
can come to my house
again soon.
                Your friend,
                Susan

McGraw-Hill School Division

At Home: Write a letter with a family member. Take turns
thinking of greetings and closings. Then choose the
greeting and closing that are most appropriate.

34

McGraw-Hill Language Arts
Grade 3, Unit 3, Verbs,
pages 166–167

10

Mixed Review

RULES

- An **action verb** shows action.
- Add **-s** or **-es** to most singular verbs in the present tense. If a verb ends with a consonant and **y,** change the **y** to **i** and add **-es.**

    My teacher | **takes** | us to the Sky Dome.

    My class | **studies** | astronomy.

- If the subject of a sentence is plural or is *I, you,* or *we,* do not add -s or -es to the verb in the present tense.

    We | **look** | through a telescope.

    I | **find** | a star right away.

Read each sentence. Write the correct form of the verb in ( ) on the line.

1. We (watch, watches) the stars in the Sky Dome. _____

2. I (explore, explores) the night sky with a big telescope. _____

3. Tim (look, looks) at the stars. _____

4. He (see, sees) many stars and planets. _____

5. Our planet (move, moves) in space. _____

6. The planets (circle, circles) the sun. _____

7. Astronomers (work, works) when it's dark. _____

8. An astronomer (study, studies)

    the position of the stars. _____

9. A new star (appear, appears)

    suddenly in the sky. _____

10. Astronomers (take, takes) photos

    of these events. _____

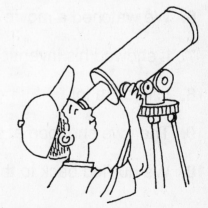

McGraw-Hill School Division

McGraw-Hill Language Arts
Grade 3, Unit 3, Verbs,
pages 168–169
10

At Home: Watch a sports event with a family member. Describe the event. Be sure to use colorful action verbs to describe what you see. Use the correct verb forms.

35

Past-Tense Verbs

> **RULES**
>
> - A **past-tense verb** tells about an action that happened already.
>   Add **-ed** to most verbs to form the past tense.
>   *We visited a science museum last week.*
> - When adding the **-ed** ending, some verbs change their spelling.
> - For verbs that end with a consonant and **y:**
>   Change the **y** to **i** before adding **-ed.**
>   *try → tried   spy → spied*
> - For verbs that end in **e:**
>   Drop the **e** and add **-ed.**
>   *close → closed   bake → baked*
> - For verbs that end with one vowel and one consonant:
>   Double the consonant and add **-ed.**
>   *hug → hugged   pat → patted*

Underline the past-tense verb in each sentence.

1. We explored the museum.

2. We stopped at every exhibit.

3. They showed us a lot about inventions.

4. The signs explained the inventions.

5. Inventions changed our lives.

6. We watched a movie about Thomas Edison.

7. It showed his invention of the light bulb.

8. I liked it a lot.

9. Then we shopped at the museum store.

10. We hurried back to the school bus just in time.

At Home: Talk with your family about what you learned or might have learned on a trip to a museum. Use past-tense verbs.

36

McGraw-Hill Language Arts
Grade 3, Unit 3, Verbs,
pages 170–171

10

McGraw-Hill School Division

Future-Tense Verbs

- A **future-tense verb** tells about an action that is going to happen. Use **will** with the action verb to tell about the future.

    *Tomorrow we **will go** on a field trip.*

    *I **will have** a great time.*

    Present Tense → *The show start**s**.*

    Past Tense → *The show start**ed**.*

    Future Tense → *The show **will start**.*

Underline the verb in each sentence. Then circle *present, past,* or *future* to tell the tense.

1. Our class will take a trip to the theater. present   past   future

2. We will watch a play. present   past   future

3. We visited the theater last year. present   past   future

4. The bus leaves early for trips. present   past   future

5. We will see "Sadako and the Thousand Paper Cranes." present   past   future

6. We will wear nice clothes. present   past   future

7. Some students will buy food there. present   past   future

8. Others will bring their own food. present   past   future

9. We will arrive home late. present   past   future

10. Everyone loves these field trips. present   past   future

McGraw-Hill Language Arts
Grade 3, Unit 3, Verbs,
pages 172–173

10

At Home: Talk with your family about a trip you would like to take some day and what you will do. Listen for future-tense verbs.

37

Combining Sentences: Verbs

┌─ **RULES** ───┐

• Join two sentences that have the same subject by **combining the predicates.**

Roxy finds leaves.

Roxy makes leaf prints.

Roxy finds leaves and makes leaf prints.

• Use the word **and** to combine the predicates.

and

Roxy gets a large crayon. ~~Roxy~~ rubs the paper.

*Roxy gets a large crayon **and** rubs the paper.*

└──┘

Use *and* to combine the predicates of each pair of sentences. Write the new sentence.

1. Our club creates art.
   Our club makes crafts.

   _____

2. Ms. Lin shows us ideas.
   Ms. Lin helps us choose one.

   _____

3. We select our materials.
   We find a place to work.

   _____

4. Jeff takes the scissors.
   Jeff cuts pieces of felt.

   _____

5. Robby reads the directions.
   Robby follows them.

   _____

At Home: Tell a family member how you made a craft item or did an art project. Use *and* to combine sentences.

38

McGraw-Hill Language Arts
Grade 3, Unit 3, Verbs,
pages 174–175

5

McGraw-Hill School Division

Mechanics and Usage:
Commas in Dates and Places

RULES

• Use a **comma** between the names of a city or town and state.

Seattle [,] *Washington*

Union City [,] *New Jersey*

• Use a **comma** between the day and the year in a date.

September 26 [,] *2001*

Write the dates and places. Put the comma in the correct place in each.

1. Gary Indiana _____

2. January 10 2005 _____

3. February 26 2004 _____

4. Carson City Nevada _____

5. Augusta Maine _____

6. April 4 1995 _____

7. Santa Fe New Mexico _____

8. January 11 2010 _____

9. Eugene Oregon _____

10. December 25 2050 _____

10 **McGraw-Hill Language Arts**
Grade 3, Unit 3, Verbs,
pages 176–177

At Home: Write the birth dates and hometowns of your
family members. Use commas where they belong.

39

Mixed Review

┌─ **RULES** ───┐

• Add **-ed** to most verbs to show action that happened in the past.

    Present   **Past**
      ↓   ↓

  I **look** at you.   I **looked** at you.

• Use *will* with action verbs to tell about something that is going to happen in the future.

    Present   **Future**
      ↓   ↓

  I **look** at you.   I **will look** at you.

• Use the word *and* to join the predicates of two sentences with the same subject.

    Marlene's plant is green. Marlene's plant grows quickly.
                ↓

    Marlene's plant is green **and** *grows quickly.*

└──┘

Read each sentence. Write the verb in the tense shown in ( ).

1. Marlene (worry, *past tense*) about her plant. _____

2. Her father (want, *past tense*) to move it. _____

3. "Your plant (grow, *future tense*) better near the light," he said.

_____

4. Marlene (lift, *past tense*) her flowerpot. _____

5. She (place, *past tense*) it on the windowsill. _____

6. The sun (shine, *future tense*) on it in the afternoon. _____

7. The plant (need, *future tense*) water. _____

8. She (sprinkle, *future tense*) it with water. _____

9. "I (give, *future tense*) it some plant food, too," she said.

_____

10. Marlene's plant (improve, *future tense*) now. _____

At Home: With a family member, make a "Past and Future" chart. On one side, write sentences with past-tense verbs. On the other, write sentences with future-tense verbs.

McGraw-Hill Language Arts
Grade 3, Unit 3, Verbs,
pages 178–179 /10

McGraw-Hill School Division

Common Errors with Subject-Verb Agreement

RULES

The **subject** and **verb** in a sentence must always agree.

- If the subject is one person or thing, then the verb must tell about one person or thing. Add *-s* or *-es* to the verb.

    This sentence is <u>not</u> correct: *My brother **pack** for the trip.*

    This sentence is correct: *My brother **packs** for the trip.*

- If the subject is more than one person or thing, then the verb must tell about more than one person or thing.

    This sentence is <u>not</u> correct: *His friends **watches**.*

    This sentence is correct: *His friends **watch**.*

- If the subject has two nouns joined by *and,* then the verb must tell about two subjects.

    This sentence is <u>not</u> correct: *Mom and I **helps**.*

    This sentence is correct: *Mom and I **help**.*

Read each sentence. Circle the verb in ( ) that agrees with the subject.

1. This spacecraft (takes, take) us to the moon.

2. The spacecraft (carries, carry) us there in just three days.

3. Our pilot (flies, fly) at top speed.

4. We (hopes, hope) to see a view of Earth.

5. I (loves, love) my home on the moon.

6. Our family (lives, live) in a domed city.

7. Dad's robot (meets, meet) us at the Moon Dock.

8. Mom (wants, want) news from her friends on Earth.

9. Our cousins (plans, plan) to visit us for the holidays.

10. My brother and I (see, sees) the Earth from our window!

McGraw-Hill Language Arts Grade 3, Unit 3, Verbs, pages 180–181

At Home: Think of a place you want to go. Write a story about it. Make sure the subjects and verbs agree, then point them out to a family member.

10 / 41

Study Skills: Note-Taking and Summarizing

┌─ **RULES** ─────────────────────────────────────┐
- One way to remember what you read is to **take notes** about the main idea and details.
- Then you can write a **summary** to state briefly the main idea and the important details.
└──┘

Read the summary. Follow the directions to write the main idea and the important facts.

   Cheetahs hunt differently from other big cats. Most big cats hunt at night. They hide themselves, wait for their prey, and then leap out. Cheetahs hunt in broad daylight. When they spot their prey, they come out in the open. When their prey starts to run, cheetahs chase them at top speed. If cheetahs have to run longer than a minute, they give up and go away.

1. Write the main-idea sentence.

_____

2. Write a sentence that tells a fact about when most big cats hunt.

_____

3. Write a sentence that tells an important fact about how most big cats hunt. _____

_____

4. Write a sentence that tells an important fact about when cheetahs hunt.

_____

_____

5. Write a sentence that tells an important fact about how cheetahs hunt.

_____

_____

_____

At Home: Find a book about an animal. With a family member, choose an interesting paragraph. Decide which sentence is the main idea. Choose another sentence that tells an important fact.

42

McGraw-Hill Language Arts
Grade 3, Unit 3, Study Skills,
pages 188–189   **5**

McGraw-Hill School Division

Vocabulary: Prefixes

- A **prefix** is a word part that is added to the beginning of a word. It changes the meaning of the base word.

Prefix		Meaning		Example	
dis-	=	opposite of	→	**dis** + connect	- disconnect
dis-	=	not	→	**dis** + honest	- dishonest
re-	=	again	→	**re** + enter	- reenter
un-	=	not	→	**un** + able	- unable
un-	=	opposite of	→	**un** + cover	- uncover

Circle the word in each row that has a prefix.

1. unlike   universe   unless

2. disk   distaste   different

3. usable   unwrap   umbrella

4. radish   radio   review

5. distrust   desert   deserve

6. reword   reason   really

7. unit   ugly   unchain

8. dipper   drink   disorder

9. resend   read   reptile

10. uncle   utter   unreal

McGraw-Hill Language Arts
Grade 3, Unit 3, Vocabulary,
pages 190–191

10

At Home: With a family member, look at advertisements in an old magazine. Find as many words as you can with the prefixes *dis-*, *re-*, and *un-*. Cut them out and make a word collage.

43

Composition: Leads and Endings

> A good **lead:**
> - gets the readers' attention and makes them want to read more.
> - may give the main idea.
>
> A good **ending:**
> - lets the readers know that the story is finished.
> - may draw a conclusion, state the main idea again, or sum up what the writer said.

Read each sentence. Write on the line if it is a **lead** or an **ending.**

1. In closing, I hope you come to my concert. _____

2. Our new park has opened, and it's fun, fun, fun! _____

3. Have you ever seen wild wolves? _____

4. Today I'll tell you about my adventure. _____

5. That was the funniest event in my life. _____

6. Finally, we all got home. _____

7. Guess what you'll see at City Center? _____

8. I am sure I'll never forget that day. _____

9. Learn to sew in three easy steps! _____

10. We have a new member in our family. _____

At Home: Look at some of your favorite storybooks. With a member of your family, read the beginnings and endings of three stories.

McGraw-Hill Language Arts
Grade 3, Unit 3, Composition,
pages 192–193

44

10

McGraw-Hill School Division

Main and Helping Verbs

RULES

- Sometimes a verb may be more than one word.
  has planned   is thinking
- The **main verb** tells what the subject does or is.
  *Our class is **going** on a picnic.*
- The **helping verb** helps the main verb show an action.
  *Our class **is** going on a picnic.*
- Here are some verbs often used as helping verbs.

have	am	was
has	is	were
had	are	will

Circle the main verb and underline the helping verb in each sentence.

1. Everyone has packed a lunch.

2. Mrs. DeWall is bringing a watermelon.

3. Mr. Lopez will plan some games.

4. Miguel and Kurt have brought a baseball.

5. Melissa and Thomas were carrying some water jugs.

6. Thomas had thrown a ball to Luis.

7. Louise was getting a drink of water.

8. I am hiding behind the tree.

9. Pete has run after a rabbit.

10. Luis and I are running after Pete.

McGraw-Hill Language Arts
Grade 3, Unit 4, Verbs,
pages 240–241
10

At Home: Ask family members what they like to do on a picnic. Write three sentences about the activities using main and helping verbs.

45

Using Helping Verbs

> **RULES**
> - Use the **helping verbs** *has, have,* and *had* to help main verbs show an action in the past.
> - Both the main verb and the helping verb must agree with the subject of the sentence.
>   *John **has** gone to the library.*
>   *Anna and Sue **have** worked on a report.*
>   *John **had** taken out two library books.*

Circle the correct helping verb to use in each sentence.

1. My class (have, has) studied insects.

2. I (had, has) written a report about bees.

3. Paul (have, had) written his report about grasshoppers.

4. We (has, have) displayed our reports in the library.

5. Other students (have, has) seen our reports.

6. The bees (have, has) built a hive.

7. A bee (have, has) collected pollen.

8. The queen bee (have, has) laid some eggs.

9. The bees (have, has) made some honey.

10. I (have, has) learned a lot about bees.

At Home: With a family member, choose an animal. Write three sentences about what the animal does. Be sure to use helping verbs with the main verbs.

46

McGraw-Hill Language Arts
Grade 3, Unit 4, Verbs,
pages 242–243 10

Linking Verbs

┌─ **RULES** ══════════════════════════════════════
│ • A **linking verb** does not show action. It connects the subject to a
│   noun or an adjective in the predicate.
│   *The monkey **is** cute.*
│ • The verb **be** is a common linking verb.
│   *Raj **is** at the zoo.*
│   *I **am** at the zoo, too.*
└──

Draw a line under each verb. Write **linking verb** or **action verb** to
describe each verb.

1. We looked into the monkey cage. _____

2. The monkeys were loud. _____

3. The littlest monkey was the cutest. _____

4. One large monkey swung from a tall tree. _____

5. He played with another monkey. _____

6. My baby brother is asleep. _____

7. I am tired, too. _____

8. Our family leaves the zoo. _____

9. We walk to our car.

   _____

10. The zoo was fun.

   _____

McGraw-Hill Language Arts
Grade 3, Unit 4, Verbs,
pages 244–245

`10`

At Home: Talk with your family about a trip you have taken.
Write three sentences about it. Underline the action or
linking verbs in each sentence.

Using Linking Verbs

RULES

- Use the linking verbs *is, am,* and *was* when the subject of the sentence is singular.

    *I **am** at camp all week.*

    *My friend Eric **is** at camp, too.*

    *Our favorite counselor **was** at camp last year.*

- Use *are* and *were* with a plural subject and *you.*

    *Eric and I **are** at camp all week.*

    *We **were** at camp last week, too.*

If the correct linking verb is used, write **correct.** If an incorrect linking verb is used, write **incorrect.**

1. Today is field day at camp. _____

2. My friend and I is in two events. _____

3. I am in the relay race. _____

4. Trevor and Casey is on the team, too. _____

5. We was the winners last year. _____

6. Some of the children were on the swim team. _____

7. I was not on the swim team. _____

8. The sun are not warm today. _____

9. The lake are very cold. _____

10. I am ready for the race. _____

At Home: With a family member, talk about what you did or would like to do on a family trip. Write three sentences **48** about these activities. Use at least one linking verb.

McGraw-Hill Language Arts Grade 3, Unit 4, Verbs, pages 246–247 10

Mechanics and Usage: Commas in a Series

RULES

• Use **commas** to separate three or more words in a series.
• Do not use a comma after the last word in a series.
  Mom, Dad, and I are going to the circus.

Write each group of words. Add commas where needed.

1. tigers elephants and horses

_____

2. clowns tightrope walkers and lion tamers

_____

3. pizza popcorn and peanuts

_____

4. bicycles tricycles and unicycles

_____

5. lions tigers and elephants

_____

6. the clowns the dogs and the ponies

_____

7. laughed cheered and clapped

_____

8. a program some popcorn and a drink

_____

9. a silly hat a balloon and a poster

_____

10. My mom my dad my sister and I

_____

McGraw-Hill Language Arts
Grade 3, Unit 4, Verbs,
pages 248–249

10

At Home: With a family member, choose a special event you attended together. Write a sentence telling three things you liked about the event. Be sure to use commas as needed.

49

Mixed Review

RULES

- The **main verb** tells what the subject is or does.
  *My family **raises** Great Danes.*

- A **helping verb** comes before the main verb. It helps the main verb show action.

          helping verb   main verb

  *Mom   **is**   **taking**   the dogs for a walk.*

- Use the helping verbs **has, have,** and **had** to help main verbs show an action in the past.

- The **linking verb** *be* does not show action.

- Use **is, am,** and **was** with singular subjects.
  *Our oldest dog **is** white with big black spots.*

- Use **are** and **were** with plural subjects and *you.*
  *The dogs **are** very well trained.*

Read each sentence. Draw a box around the linking verb. Draw a line under a main verb with a helping verb.

1. The big event each year is the dog show.

2. We are taking our Great Danes in a van.

3. A trainer is trotting them around the ring.

4. By this time last year, our dog Brutus had won first place.

5. My sister and I are taking turns grooming our dogs.

6. I was brushing Brutus before the show.

7. He is wearing a beautiful silver collar with gold stars on it.

8. Other kinds of dogs are at the dog show.

9. This morning I was watching the beagles with their long, floppy ears.

10. The collies are always so loud!

At Home: With a family member, write five things a dog can do. Use main verbs with helping verbs, linking verbs, and action verbs.

50

McGraw-Hill Language Arts
Grade 3, Unit 4, Verbs,
pages 250–251

/10

Irregular Verbs

> **RULES**
> - An irregular verb has a special spelling to show the past tense.
> - Some irregular verbs have a special spelling when used with a helping verb.
>
> | Present | Past | With Helping Verbs |
> |---------|------|--------------------|
> | *come* | *came* | *had, has,* or *have come* |
> | *do* | *did* | *had, has,* or *have done* |
> | *say* | *said* | *had, has,* or *have said* |
> | *go* | *went* | *had, has,* or *have gone* |
> | *run* | *ran* | *had, has,* or *have run* |
> | *see* | *saw* | *had, has,* or *have seen* |
> | *drive* | *drove* | *had, has,* or *have driven* |

Circle the past tense of each verb in ( ). Then write it on the line.

1. We (go, went) to the beach. _____

2. We (see, saw) lots of shells. _____

3. Two boys (ran, run) by us. _____

4. We (said, say) hello to them. _____

5. The boys (do, did) a double-take. _____

6. We (had seen, see) the boys before. _____

7. Those boys (had come, come) last summer. _____

8. They (come, came) to the beach with their parents. _____

9. We (had gone, go) fishing with them last year. _____

10. We (has gone, went) fishing in their boat. _____

McGraw-Hill Language Arts
Grade 3, Unit 4, Verbs,
pages 252–253

10

At Home: Ask a family member to tell about a suprise meeting. Write about it, using at least two irregular verbs.

51

More Irregular Verbs

┌─ **RULES** ───┐

- **Irregular verbs** do not add **-ed** to show past tense.
- Irregular verbs have special spellings in the past tense and when they are used with a helping verb.

Present	Past	With Helping Verbs
begin	*began*	**had, has,** or *have begun*
eat	*ate*	**had, has,** or *have eaten*
give	*gave*	**had, has,** or *have given*
grow	*grew*	**had, has,** or *have grown*
sing	*sang*	**had, has,** or *have sung*
bring	*brought*	**had, has,** or *have brought*

└──┘

Circle the irregular verb in each sentence.

1. Grandpa had given me a zucchini plant.

2. The zucchini plant has grown very large.

3. The zucchinis began to sprout.

4. I brought the zucchinis to my mother.

5. We have eaten a lot of zucchinis.

6. I have sung to my plant.

7. I have given my plant vitamins.

8. My plant has grown large.

9. I brought some of my zucchinis to a sick friend.

10. I gave some seeds to my friend.

At Home: Write some sentences about a plant. Be sure to include at least one irregular verb in your writing. Show your writing to a family member.

McGraw-Hill Language Arts
Grade 3, Unit 4, Verbs,
pages 254–255

10

McGraw-Hill School Division

Contractions with *Not*

RULES

- A **contraction** is a shortened form of two words. In a contraction, one or more letters are left out.
- Use an **apostrophe (')** to take the place of the missing letter or letters.

have not = haven't	is not = isn't
are not = aren't	was not = wasn't
cannot = can't	do not = don't
does not = doesn't	were not = weren't

- The word **won't** is a special contraction. In this contraction, the spelling of **will** changes.

  will not = won't

Look at the words in the first column. Then circle the correct contractions formed from the words.

1. is not   isn't   aren't   can't

2. should not   won't   didn't   shouldn't

3. will not   wouldn't   won't   wasn't

4. were not   weren't   wasn't   hadn't

5. had not   hasn't   hadn't   haven't

6. are not   aren't   can't   couldn't

7. does not   don't   didn't   doesn't

8. did not   can't   doesn't   didn't

9. has not   hadn't   hasn't   haven't

10. was not   wasn't   weren't   won't

McGraw-Hill Language Arts
Grade 3, Unit 4, Verbs,
pages 256–257
10

At Home: With a family member, think of three rules you have in your home. Write these rules using contractions.

53

Combining Sentences: Verbs

┌─ **RULES** ───
│ • Two sentences with the **same subject** can be combined.
│ • Use the word **and** to join the predicates.
│   *We saw the museum.*
│   *We went inside.*
│   *We saw the museum **and** went inside.*
└──

Write each pair of sentences as one sentence on the lines below.
Use the word *and* to combine the predicates.

1. We saw a huge model airplane.
   We walked up close to it.

   _____

   _____

2. A man talked about the Wright brothers.
   A man described the first airplane.

   _____

   _____

3. The Wright brothers read many books.
   The Wright brothers did many experiments.

   _____

   _____

4. They built an airplane.
   They brought it to Kitty Hawk.

   _____

   _____

5. The airplane lifted off the ground.
   The airplane flew for 59 seconds.

   _____

   _____

At Home: Write two sentences about something you would
like to invent. Combine the predicates of the sentences.
54   Show your new sentence to a family member.

McGraw-Hill Language Arts
Grade 3, Unit 4, Verbs,
pages 258–259   **5**

McGraw-Hill School Division

Mechanics and Usage: Apostrophes

RULES

- Use an **apostrophe (')** with nouns or plural nouns to show **possession.**

    The sun's rays   the boys' club

- Add **'s** to **singular nouns** or plural nouns that do not end in -**s.**

    dog's cage   children's smiles

- Add an apostrophe to **plural nouns** ending in -**s.**

    rabbits' noses   cats' whiskers

- Use an apostrophe in a **contraction** to show where letters are missing.

    did not → didn't

    is not → isn't

Underline each word that contains an apostrophe. Write **possession** or **contraction** to show how the apostrophe is used.

1. Shasta's bed is in the corner of my room.

   _____

2. Aren't puppies fun in the morning?

   _____

3. I can't take her to school with me.

   _____

4. She plays in our neighbor's yard during the day.

   _____

5. She isn't happy until I get back home.

   _____

McGraw-Hill School Division

At Home: With your family, make a *Do and Don't* list for caring for a family pet. Spell the contraction *don't* correctly each time you use it.

Mixed Review

RULES

- **Irregular verbs** have a special spelling for the past tense and when used with *have, has,* or *had.*
    - go/went/gone   do/did/done   come/came/come
- Some verbs join with ***not*** to form contractions. An **apostrophe** (') shows where one or more letters have been left out.
- Use an **apostrophe** with nouns to show **possession.** Add ***'s*** to singular nouns or plural nouns that do not end in *s.*

Write the correct past form of each verb in ( ). Add apostrophes where they are missing from other words.

1. My rabbit, Scooter, (run) away once. We couldnt find him.   _____

2. We (drive) all over the neighborhood looking for him.   _____

3. My rabbit (do) not come home. Scooters cage was empty.   _____

4. I (begin) to wonder where he might be.   _____

5. Dad (say), "Lets look in the woods."   _____

6. Then a neighbor (give) us information.   _____

7. He (see) Scooter in a nearby garden. The gardens fence was broken.   _____

8. Scooter wasnt shy! He (eat) our neighbor's lettuce!   _____

9. The neighbor (find) him after two days.   _____

10. Scooter never (go) away again.   _____

At Home: Ask a family member to tell something that happened to a pet. Listen for the irregular verbs *go, do,* and *come.* Write the forms that you hear.

56

McGraw-Hill Language Arts
Grade 3, Unit 4, Verbs,
pages 262–263

10

McGraw-Hill School Division

Common Errors with Past-Tense Verbs

╒═ RULES ═

- Add **-ed** to most verbs to show past tense.

- Some verbs have special spellings to show the past tense. It is important to learn which verbs are irregular.

- Some irregular verbs have a different spelling when used with a helping verb.

Verb	Past	With *have, has,* or *had*
see	*saw*	*seen*
come	*came*	*come*
bring	*brought*	*brought*
eat	*ate*	*eaten*
give	*gave*	*given*
go	*went*	*gone*
say	*said*	*said*
begin	*began*	*begun*
run	*ran*	*run*

Circle the irregular verb in each sentence.

1. Winter has brought a delightful surprise.

2. Snowflakes have begun to fall.

3. We saw icicles in the trees.

4. We brought our sled to the park.

5. We went down the big hill.

6. My family went to our cabin.

7. My uncle came to the cabin, too.

8. Father brought some firewood.

9. Grandmother gave us chestnuts to roast.

10. We ate by the fire.

McGraw-Hill Language Arts
Grade 3, Unit 4, Verbs,
pages 264–265

At Home: Think about some fun things to do in the snow.
With your family, write three sentences using irregular
verbs to tell about your ideas.

57

McGraw-Hill School Division

Study Skills: Graphs

RULES

- A **graph** is a diagram that shows the relationship between two or more things. You can use a graph to compare information.

- A **bar graph** uses bars to compare information.

- A **circle graph** compares parts of a whole.

- A **line graph** can show changes over a period of time.

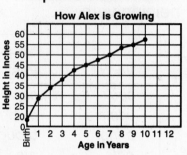

Look at the graphs above. Which graph (bar graph, circle graph, or line graph) would help you answer each question? Write the name of the kind of graph on the line.

1. How does Alex spend his time each day?

   _____

2. How tall was Alex at six years old?

   _____

3. How fast can Alex sing the alphabet?

   _____

4. How many inches did Alex grow between the ages of 1 and 3 years old?

   _____

5. How many hours does Alex spend on homework?

   _____

6. How many hours does Alex spend at school?

   _____

7. How long does it take Alex to hop ten times?

   _____

8. How much time does Alex spend watching television?

   _____

9. Does Alex spend more time doing homework or playing?

   _____

10. At what age was Alex 50 inches tall?

   _____

At Home: Ask family members to help you make a graph of how many inches you have grown since you were born.

58

McGraw-Hill Language Arts
Grade 3, Unit 4, Study Skills,
pages 272–273

10

McGraw-Hill School Division

Vocabulary: Suffixes

- A **suffix** is a word part added to the end of a base word. A **suffix** changes the meaning of a base word.

sing + er = singer → A singer is a person who sings.

slow + ly = slowly → To move slowly means to move in a slow way.

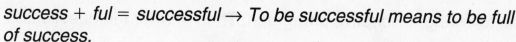

I move slowly.

success + ful = successful → To be successful means to be full of success.

Suffixes	Example	Meaning
-er	dan<u>cer</u>	one who dances
-or	govern<u>or</u>	one who governs
-less	help<u>less</u>	without help
-able	fix<u>able</u>	able to be fixed
-ly	slowly	in a slow way
-ful	hop<u>eful</u>	full of hope

A. Draw lines to match the words on the left with their meanings on the right.

1. understandable   one who talks
2. thankless   full of joy
3. sharply   able to be understood
4. talker   without thanks
5. joyful   in a sharp way

B. Circle the word in each row that has a suffix.

6. teachable	target	telephone
7. polite	photographer	prairie
8. sentence	sunless	sail
9. jealous	jungle	faithful
10. darkly	dictionary	deserve

McGraw-Hill Language Arts
Grade 3, Unit 4, Vocabulary,
pages 274–275

10

At Home: Take turns with a family member naming as many jobs as you can that end with the suffix *-er* or *-or*.
(Examples: painter, farmer, actor, editor, teacher, firefighter.)

59

Composition: Writing Descriptions

A **description** can be about persons, places, or things.
Descriptive paragraphs have:

• a **main-idea** sentence.

• **sensory details** that describe how things look, taste, smell, sound, and feel.

• an **order that makes sense.**

Read the following descriptive paragraph. Then answer the questions.

In the summer, the Rocky Mountains are a popular place for campers and hikers. These mountains are the perfect place to hike because of the bright blue sky, snowy mountain peaks, and rolling green hills. When hikers climb high above the campsites, the fresh breeze blows gently, and the sweet smell of wildflowers is in the air. It is very quiet except for the wind in the trees and the rushing of small streams over rocks. After spending a day high in the majestic Rocky Mountains, hikers look forward to another visit to this beautiful and peaceful place.

1. Draw a line under the sentence that tells the main idea.

2. What does the main-idea sentence describe?

_____

3. Which of your five senses do "very quiet," "wind in the trees," and "rushing of small streams" tell about?

_____

4. Which words tell you how the mountains look?

_____

5. Which words describe the sense of smell?

_____

At Home: With a family member, think of a beautiful place. Write five sentences describing the place. Use sensory words for all your senses.

McGraw-Hill Language Arts
Grade 3, Unit 4, Composition,
pages 276–277

5

Pronouns

RULES

- A **pronoun** is a word that takes the place of one or more nouns.
  Adam works hard. → *He works hard.*
- A pronoun must match the noun or nouns that it replaces.
- To replace a single person, place, or thing, use a **singular pronoun.**
  singular pronouns = *I, you, he, she, it, me, him, her*
  Liz brought a violin. → *Liz brought it.*
- To replace more than one person, place, or thing, use a **plural pronoun.**
  plural pronouns = *we, you, they, us, them*
  ***Leroy and Alice** are hungry.* → ***They** are hungry.*

Read each sentence. Tell whether the underlined pronoun is singular or plural.

1. Julio watches <u>them</u> play. _____

2. <u>He</u> wants to play basketball, too. _____

3. <u>They</u> do not need any more players on the team. _____

4. Throw the ball to <u>me</u>. _____

5. <u>It</u> goes over the fence. _____

6. <u>He</u> lost the ball. _____

7. Now <u>we</u> can't play basketball. _____

8. <u>I</u> have a baseball. _____

9. All the children now want <u>him</u> to play. _____

10. Julio can play baseball with <u>us</u>. _____

McGraw-Hill Language Arts
Grade 3, Unit 5, Pronouns,
pages 322–323

10

At Home: Scramble the letters of five pronouns. Ask family members to tell what pronouns they are.

Subject Pronouns

┌─ **RULES** ═══
│ • A **subject pronoun** is used as the subject of a sentence.
│
│   Singular subject pronouns → *I, you, he, she, it*
│
│   Plural subject pronouns → *we, you, they*
│
│ • A subject pronoun takes the place of the subject of a sentence.
│
│ | **Rita** | *opened the letter.* → | **She** | *opened the letter.*
│
│ | **Kate and Tom** | *met us.* → | **They** | *met us.*
└──

Write the subject pronoun of each sentence.

1. They wake up early on Saturday.   _____

2. She wants to go to the beach.   _____

3. He wants to go to the swimming pool.   _____

4. We want to play baseball in the park.   _____

5. You can go to the beach tomorrow.   _____

6. I will go to the park with my friends today.   _____

7. It is too crowded today.   _____

8. He decides to go to the pool, instead.   _____

9. They have fun at the pool and at the park.   _____

10. We all go to the beach the next day.   _____

McGraw-Hill School Division

At Home: Think of an outdoor activity you enjoy. Use
subject pronouns in at least two sentences to tell a family
62 member about the activity.

McGraw-Hill Language Arts
Grade 3, Unit 5, Pronouns,
pages 324–325

/ 10

Object Pronouns

> **RULES**
>
> • An **object pronoun** replaces one or more nouns in the predicate part of a sentence.
>
> • Use an **object pronoun** after an action verb, or after words such as *for, at, of, with, in,* and *to.*
>
> Singular Object Pronouns → *me, you, him, her, it*
>
> Plural Object Pronouns → *us, you, them*
>
> Rina will buy | **the notebooks** | .
>
> Rina will buy | **them** | .

Write the object pronoun of each sentence.

1. Anna and Justin planned to visit us today. _____

2. We waited for them all afternoon. _____

3. Justin called me at three o'clock. _____

4. He explained what happened to them. _____

5. The tire on Anna's bike had a nail in it. _____

6. Justin knew how to help her. _____

7. They can fix it at the gas station. _____

8. They took the bikes and walked them to the gas station together. _____

9. Justin left a message for you. _____

10. You can meet him at four o'clock. _____

McGraw-Hill Language Arts
Grade 3, Unit 5, Pronouns,
pages 326–327
10

At Home: Ask a family member to tell about visiting a friend. Listen for object pronouns. Make a list of the object pronouns you hear.

63

Mechanics and Usage:
Using *I* and *Me*

┌─ **RULES** ─────────────────────────────────────┐

- Use the pronouns *I* and *me* to write about yourself. Always write the pronoun *I* with a capital letter.
- Use *I* in the subject of a sentence.
    I have work to do.
- Use *me* after an action verb and after words such as *in, into, to, with, by,* or *at.*
    *My friends help **me**.*
- When you talk about yourself and another person, name yourself last.
- To help you decide whether to use *I* or *me,* try the sentence leaving out the other person.
    *Ms. Kemper brought pencils for ~~Ellie and~~ **me**.*
    *~~Joel and~~ **I** arranged the chairs.*

└───┘

Circle the pronoun in ( ) that is correct in each sentence.

1. (I, Me) must read a book about animals.

2. Leroy comes with Kim and (I, me) to the library.

3. Leroy finds a book about snakes for (I, me).

4. (I, Me) do not like snakes.

5. Kim and (I, me) look for another book.

6. Leroy calls (I, me) over to the bookshelf.

7. Now he shows (I, me) some books about dogs.

8. (I, Me) would like to read about dogs.

9. Kim looks at the book with Leroy and (I, me).

10. Leroy, Kim, and (I, me) will all read about dogs.

At Home: Ask a family member to tell about a time someone was helpful to him or her. Listen for sentences that use *I* or *me*, and write them down.

64

McGraw-Hill Language Arts
Grade 3, Unit 5, Pronouns,
pages 328–329   10

Mixed Review

┌─ **RULES** ───┐

• A **pronoun** takes the place of one or more nouns.

• A **pronoun** must match the noun it replaces.

• Use a **subject pronoun** as the subject of a sentence.

> | *Angela* | *rides every afternoon.*
>
> | *She* | *rides every afternoon.*

• Use an **object pronoun** after an action verb or after words such as *for, at, of, with,* and *to.*

> *Mr. Ramirez leads the horses to* | *Angela and me* |.
>
> *Mr. Ramirez leads the horses to* | *us* |.

└───┘

Read each sentence. Circle the word that tells whether the underlined pronoun is a subject pronoun or an object pronoun.

1. Luis invited <u>me</u> to the ranch.   subject   object

2. <u>He</u> and Manuel train horses there.   subject   object

3. The boys' mother waved to <u>us</u>.   subject   object

4. <u>She</u> polishes all of the saddles.   subject   object

5. The white horse belongs to <u>her</u>.   subject   object

6. Mrs. Ramirez let <u>me</u> ride her horse.   subject   object

7. <u>They</u> brought three horses outside.   subject   object

8. Luis helped <u>him</u> get on the horse.   subject   object

9. <u>He</u> knew exactly what to do.   subject   object

10. <u>We</u> rode toward the mountains.   subject   object

10 **McGraw-Hill Language Arts**
Grade 3, Unit 5, Pronouns,
pages 330–331

At Home: With a family member, plan a trip you would like to take.
List things your family could do for fun. Write a few sentences
about the trip, using *I, we, he, she,* and *they* correctly.

65

Pronoun-Verb Agreement

RULES

- A **present-tense verb** must agree with its **subject pronoun.**

- Add **-s** to most action verbs in the present tense when you use the pronouns *he, she,* and *it.*

- Do not add **-s** to an action verb in the present tense when you use the pronouns *I, we, you,* and *they.*

    She plays inside.

    They play inside.

Circle the action verb in ( ) that is correct in each sentence.

1. It (rain, rains) for hours.

2. Kendra (want, wants) to play.

3. I (call, calls) her on the phone.

4. We (talk, talks) for awhile.

5. "You can (come, comes) to my house," I tell her.

6. Kendra (ask, asks) her mom and dad.

7. They (say, says) she can come.

8. We (meet, meets) on the corner of my street.

9. I (bring, brings) my umbrella.

10. She (wear, wears) her raincoat.

McGraw-Hill School Division

At Home: With a family member, draw a picture of something you do with your family. Take turns describing the picture. Use pronoun-verb agreement.

McGraw-Hill Language Arts
Grade 3, Unit 5, Pronouns,
pages 332–333

10

Possessive Pronouns

RULES

- A **possessive pronoun** takes the place of a possessive noun. It shows who or what owns something.

  The children's playroom is at the end of the hall.

  Their playroom is at the end of the hall.

- Some possessive pronouns are used before nouns.

my	your	his	her	its	our	your	their

  my book   **her** raincoat   **their** project

- Other possessive pronouns can stand alone.

mine	yours	his	hers	its	ours	theirs

  *These books are **mine.*** *Which sandwich is **yours?***

Circle the possessive pronoun in each sentence.

1. My little brother Chad was playing in the den.

2. Chad was playing with his soccer ball.

3. The ball hit our computer by accident.

4. My mom was not happy at all.

5. Mom took his soccer ball away.

6. Our rule is "No soccer in the house."

7. Now I will have to use the computer at my school.

8. Its screen is bigger than the computer at home.

9. Mom likes her keyboard much better, though.

10. Mom and Dad will have theirs repaired.

McGraw-Hill Language Arts
Grade 3, Unit 5, Pronouns,
pages 334–335
`10`

At Home: Ask family members what uses they have or would have for a computer. Use a possessive pronoun to write their answers.

67

Pronoun-Verb Contractions

RULES

- A **contraction** is a shortened form of two words. There are many pronoun-verb contractions.
- Use an **apostrophe (')** to replace the letter or letters that are left out.

  ***You are** late for school.* → ***You're** late for school.*
- Here are some contractions.

he's = he + is or he + has	*they're = they + are*	*he'll = he + will*
she's = she + is or she + has	*I've = I + have*	*she'll = she + will*
it's = it + is or it + has	*you've = you + have*	*we'll = we + will*
I'm = I + am	*we've = we + have*	*you'll = you + will*
you're = you + are	*they've = they + have*	*it'll = it + will*
we're = we + are	*I'll = I + will*	*they'll = they + will*

Circle the two words that each contraction stands for.

1. they'll	they will	they can	they are
2. she's	he will	she is	she will
3. you're	you is	they are	you are
4. it's	it are	it is	it will
5. I'm	I am	I will	I is
6. they're	they will	they is	they are
7. you've	you have	you will	we have
8. he'll	he is	he will	it is
9. we're	we are	we will	we have
10. you'll	you are	you have	you will

At Home: Make a set of cards with the two parts of a contraction on one side and the contraction on the other. Take turns with a family member looking at the two words and saying the contraction.

McGraw-Hill Language Arts
Grade 3, Unit 5, Pronouns,
pages 336–337 / 10

McGraw-Hill School Division

Mechanics and Usage:
Contractions and Possessive Pronouns

> **RULES**
>
> - Be careful not to confuse possessive pronouns with contractions.
>
> - In a **contraction,** an **apostrophe (')** takes the place of the letters that are left out.
>
>   ***They are*** *going to the zoo.* → ***They're*** *going to the zoo.*
>
> - **Possessive pronouns** do not have apostrophes.
>
>   *Are they driving in **their** car?*

Circle the contraction or possessive pronoun in each sentence. Write whether it is a possessive pronoun or a contraction.

1. They're moving to another city.   _____

2. Their house is for sale.   _____

3. It's a big house.   _____

4. We liked to play in its big yard.   _____

5. Your family went to see the house.   _____

6. Do you think you're going to buy the house?   _____

7. It's great that you will live in that house.   _____

8. They're going to get you a big dog now.   _____

9. It will be their present to you and your sister.   _____

10. Its size is not important since the yard is big. _____

At Home: Write these sentence starters on index cards: *They're eating _____ . He's eating his _____ . She's eating her _____ .* Take turns completing each card as your family eats a meal together.

Mixed Review

┌─ **RULES** ──────────────────────────────
│ • A **possessive pronoun** shows who or what owns something.
│   *Jake and Lil bought this car. It is **their** car.*
│
│ • A **contraction** is a shortened form of two words. An **apostrophe** (')
│   replaces the letters that are left out.
│   *Tomorrow **they're** driving to the city.*
│
│ • Do not confuse possessive pronouns with contractions.
│
│   possessive pronoun → | **Its** | *engine is quiet.*
│
│   contraction → | **It's** | *a bright-red car.*
└──

Read each sentence. Write the correct form of the possessive
pronoun or the contraction in ( ) on the line.

1. The king asked her to come to (he's, his) castle. _____

2. He said, "(I've, Ive) got a special room
   prepared for you, filled with straw." _____

3. "(I'm, Im) expecting this straw to become gold
   by tomorrow." _____

4. "(You'll, Youll) need some help," said a
   mysterious little man. _____

5. "In exchange for (your, you're) necklace, I'll
   spin the straw," he said. _____

6. The next day, the king could hardly believe
   (he's, his) eyes! _____

7. (Her, Hers) room was full of gold! _____

8. The little man said, "In return for the gold, you
   must guess (my, mine) name." _____

9. "(Isn't, Isnt) your name Rumpelstiltskin?" she asked. _____

10. The mysterious little man snapped (his, he's)
    fingers and disappeared. _____

At Home: With a family member, make some plans for the
weekend. Write about your plans using sentences that
70 begin with the contractions *You'll* and *I'll*.

McGraw-Hill Language Arts
Grade 3, Unit 5, Pronouns,
pages 340–341 10

Common Errors with Pronouns

┌─ **RULES** ───┐

Be sure to use the right subject and object pronouns.

- Use a **subject pronoun** as the subject of a sentence.

  This sentence is <u>not</u> correct: *Lin and **me** had a special day yesterday.*

  This sentence is correct: *Lin and **I** had a special day yesterday.*

- Use an **object pronoun** after an action verb or words such as *for, at, of, with,* and *to.*

  This sentence is <u>not</u> correct: *I went to the circus and the zoo with **she**.*

  This sentence is correct: *I went to the circus and the zoo with **her**.*

└──┘

Read each sentence. Circle the correct pronoun.

1. Lin bought _____ a ticket to the circus.   me   I

2. The trapeze artists flew back and forth above _____ .   us   we

3. _____ watched a man pull pretty white birds out of a hat.   Him   I

4. Then _____ saw clowns climb out of a tiny car.   them   we

5. _____ did lots of funny tricks.   They   Her

6. After lunch _____ went to the zoo.   we   us

7. _____ watched a woman feed a baby tiger with a bottle.   I   Me

8. _____ is a zookeeper.   She   Her

9. The baby tiger looked straight at Lin and _____ .   I   me

10. Then the baby tiger curled up next to _____ and fell asleep.   she   her

10 **McGraw-Hill Language Arts** **Grade 3, Unit 5, Pronouns,** **pages 342–343**   **At Home:** With a family member, cut out five pictures from old magazines. Write a sentence about each picture, using pronouns.

71

Study Skills: Encyclopedia

┌─ **RULES** ──────────────────────────────────

- An **encyclopedia** contains information about people, places, and things.

  Thomas Jefferson   Idaho   bicycles
  Harriet Tubman   Yosemite   frogs

- Each **volume** in an encyclopedia is arranged in alphabetical order according to the letter or letters on its spine. The volumes are numbered to keep them in order.

- The **index** lists the topics in alphabetical order.

- An **encyclopedia on CD-ROM** contains on a computer disk all the information in a set of encyclopedias.

└──

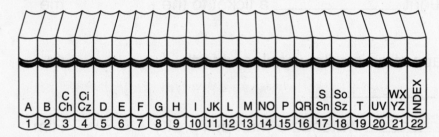

Draw a circle around the correct encyclopedia volume for each topic.

1. robots	13	16	9	**6.** England	6	5	2
2. New Zealand	14	18	12	**7.** glaciers	7	15	8
3. Cherokee	3	5	4	**8.** kangaroo	11	9	14
4. beach	6	2	9	**9.** Montana	14	13	12
5. wombat	21	12	18	**10.** aardvark	2	5	1

At Home: Write the names of several animals. With a family member, use this page to find the encyclopedia volume that has information on each animal.

McGraw-Hill Language Arts
Grade 3, Unit 5, Study Skills,
pages 350–351

10

McGraw-Hill School Division

Vocabulary: Homophones

Homophones are words that sound alike but have different spellings and different meanings.

Here are some examples of homophones:

bee, be	A _bee_ flew into my room. I hope I won't _be_ stung.
nose, knows	Her _nose_ is sunburned. She _knows_ why it hurts.
eight, ate	There were _eight_ apples before Wanda _ate_ one of them.

Read aloud the word in the first column. Circle the word in each sentence that sounds the same as this word.

1. **ate**   You can make this breakfast in eight minutes.

2. **hi**   Get a mixing bowl down from the high shelf.

3. **beet**   Beat eggs and milk in the bowl.

4. **for**   Scramble the four eggs in a pan.

5. **plane**   Do you like your eggs plain or with cheese?

6. **sum**   Cook some bacon in another pan.

7. **bred**   Toast a few slices of bread.

8. **poor**   Who will pour the orange juice?

9. **eye**   I will get the glasses.

10. **two**   Please can you set the table, too.

McGraw-Hill Language Arts
Grade 3, Unit 5, Vocabulary,
pages 352–353

At Home: Make an illustrated chart of five homophones.
Show your chart to a family member. Explain that these
words sound the same but are spelled differently.

73

10

Composition: Outlining

- An **outline** is a way of organizing ideas you will include in your writing.
- Write the **topic** at the top of the outline.
- List the first **main idea** you plan to include and give it a number. Use a Roman numeral followed by a period.
- Next, list **supporting details** under the main idea. Give each detail a letter.
- Then, list your next main idea and add details as before.
- Ideas written in an outline do not need to be complete sentences. They can be words, phrases, questions, or sentence fragments.

Read the beginning of an outline below. Read the detail sentences. Then draw a line under five detail sentences that belong under the main idea of the outline.

Topic: Bluebirds
I. What do bluebirds eat?

A. Like to eat insects

B. Build nests in tree holes

C. Will eat berries

D. Fly south in the winter

E. Sometimes eat grapes

F. Will eat beetles

G. Some of them eat caterpillars

At Home: Write the topic "Healthy Foods That Taste Good." Ask a family member to help you list five foods that belong under the main idea.

74

McGraw-Hill Language Arts
Grade 3, Unit 5, Composition,
pages 354–355

5

Adjectives That Tell *What Kind*

RULES

• An **adjective** is a word that describes a noun.
Some adjectives tell **what kind** of person, place, or thing the noun is.

*Today is a **special** day.*

↑
tells what kind

The underlined word in each sentence is an adjective. Circle the noun it describes.

1. A <u>large</u> crowd waits for the parade.

2. Ben buys a <u>green</u> balloon.

3. I see <u>colorful</u> flags.

4. <u>Funny</u> clowns make us laugh.

5. The <u>shiny</u> horns play a march.

6. We hear the <u>loud</u> horn.

7. The scouts wear <u>new</u> uniforms.

8. <u>Brown</u> horses prance by.

9. The <u>noisy</u> crowd claps and waves.

10. The <u>long</u> parade finally ends.

At Home: With a family member, take turns describing a family float you might make for a parade. Use adjectives that tell *what kind*.

Adjectives That Tell *How Many*

RULES

- An **adjective** is a word that describes a noun.
- Some adjectives tell **how many.**

    Three *children are good friends.*
         ↑
  tells how many

    *They do **many** things together.*
              ↑
         tells how many

Read each sentence. Circle the adjective that describes the underlined noun.

1. One <u>day</u> we play inside.

2. Nuna suggests several <u>things</u> to do.

3. We choose one <u>game</u> to play.

4. The game board has many <u>squares</u>.

5. Several <u>squares</u> will trap a player.

6. Few <u>players</u> miss all the traps.

7. Many <u>cards</u> are in a small pile.

8. Nuna draws one <u>card</u>.

9. Nuna moves four <u>squares</u>.

10. Luis has two <u>turns</u> in a row.

11. Mary is behind the other two <u>players</u>.

12. Luis lands on three <u>traps</u>.

13. Nuna also lands on a few <u>traps</u>.

14. We play the game several <u>times</u>.

15. Mary wins three <u>times</u>.

At Home: Play a game with family members. Then name adjectives that tell how many can play and how long the game takes.

76

McGraw-Hill Language Arts
Grade 3, Unit 6, Adjectives and Adverbs,
pages 400–401

15

McGraw-Hill School Division

Articles

RULES
- **Articles** are special adjectives. The words *a, an,* and *the* are articles.
- Use *a* before singular nouns that begin with a consonant.
  a nest
- Use *an* before singular nouns that begin with a vowel.
  an apple
- Use *the* before singular nouns and plural nouns.
  the squirrel   ***the*** squirrels

Circle the correct article in ( ) to complete each sentence.

1. Do any wild animals live in (the, an) city?

2. You might have (a, an) animal living near you.

3. At night, deer might come from (a, an) park or woods.

4. (The, An) deer might nibble the plants in your garden.

5. (A, An) raccoon might live under a porch.

6. Raccoons will raid (an, the) garbage cans.

7. Squirrels live in (a, an) tree near your house.

8. (A, An) owl might also live in the tree.

9. Mice build nests in (a, the) grass.

10. In the winter, mice may come into (an, the) house.

McGraw-Hill School Division

Adjectives That Compare

RULES
• You can use **adjectives** to compare two or more nouns.
• Add **-er** to an adjective to compare two nouns.
*Today's game was **longer** than last week's game.*
• Add **-est** to compare more than two nouns.
*Sue is the **greatest** player on our team.*

Write each sentence. Use the correct form of the adjective in ( ).

1. Alice is the (new) team member.

_____

2. Mia is the (fast) runner in our class.

_____

3. Bet's kick was (longer, longest) than Kevin's.

_____

4. She kicked to her (near) teammate.

_____

5. That player is (quick) than I am.

_____

6. The coach's whistle is (loud) than mine.

_____

7. The wind is (calm) than it was at noon.

_____

8. The new field is (smooth) than the old one.

_____

9. That team is the (strong) team in town.

_____

10. Our team's score was the (low) of all.

_____

At Home: Talk about a favorite game with a family member. Use adjectives to compare the action in the game.

78

McGraw-Hill Language Arts
Grade 3, Unit 6, Adjectives and Adverbs,
pages 404–405

10

McGraw-Hill School Division

Spelling Adjectives That Compare

> ## RULES
>
> Some adjectives change their spelling when **-er** or **-est** is added.
> - When **the adjective ends in a consonant sound and y,** change the **y** to **i** and add **-er** or **-est.**
>   *shaggy, shaggier, shaggiest*
> - When **the adjective ends in e,** drop the **e** and add **-er** or **-est.**
>   *nice, nicer, nicest*
> - For **adjectives that have a single vowel sound before a final consonant,** double the final consonant and add **-er** or **-est.**
>   *big, bigger, biggest*

Write the correct spelling of each adjective when the ending is added.

1. happy + er _____

2. tan + er _____

3. pale + er _____

4. shy + er _____

5. gentle + er _____

6. furry + est _____

7. noisy + est _____

8. pretty + est _____

9. slim + est _____

10. cute + est _____

McGraw-Hill Language Arts
Grade 3, Unit 6, Adjectives and Adverbs,
pages 406–407
10

At Home: Show the words *shaggiest, shiest,* and *noisiest* to a family member. Take turns making up sentences with these words.

79

Mechanics and Usage: Using Commas

RULES

- When you read, commas tell you when to pause.
- Use a comma **after the name of a person** being spoken to.
  Lien, did you have a good time?
- Use a comma after words like **yes** and **no** when they begin a sentence.
  Yes, I had a wonderful time.

Add a comma where it belongs in each sentence.

1. Mom is that the telephone ringing?

2. Yes can you answer it?

3. No my hands are sticky.

4. Lien Pat wants to talk with you.

5. Pat I was just thinking about you.

6. Lien can you do something special with us tomorrow?

7. Yes I would like to do that.

8. Okay that is great. We are driving to the mountains, and we will hike along Sandy River.

9. Lien Sandy River is beautiful. Have you ever seen it?

10. No I have only seen pictures of it.

11. Lien I hope you can come.

12. Pat I'll ask my mother.

13. Mom may I go on a hike and picnic with Pat and her family?

14. Yes it sounds like a wonderful day.

15. Pat I will bring my camera, too.

At Home: With a family member, write a conversation between two friends planning a trip. Use their names at the beginning of sentences.

80

McGraw-Hill Language Arts
Grade 3, Unit 6, Adjectives and Adverbs,
pages 408–409

15

McGraw-Hill School Division

Mixed Review

RULES

- The article **an** goes before singular nouns that begin with a vowel. The article **a** goes before singular nouns that begin with a consonant.

    *I saw **an** <u>owl</u> in the tree.*

    *Did you ever see **a** <u>duck</u> in a tree?*

- The article **the** goes before singular and plural nouns.

    ***The** <u>ducks</u> don't land in trees.*

- In a sentence in which you speak to someone by name, place a **comma** after the person's name.

    Mrs. Curry, do these ducks live in the pond all year?

- A comma goes after **yes** and **no** when they begin a sentence.

    Yes, they do.

For each sentence, circle the correct article. Write it on the line. Add commas where they belong.

1. Mrs. Curry are you going to feed _____   the   a
   ducks at the pond?

2. Yes I have _____ loaf of bread for them.   an   a

3. Fred do you want _____ piece of bread?   a   an

4. No I brought _____ orange.   a   an

5. Ducks don't like _____ taste of oranges.   a   the

6. Laura please don't splash _____ water.   the   an

7. That duck has _____ long beak.   an   a

8. Mrs. Curry may I give it _____ piece   a   the
   of bread?

9. Yes here is _____ crust.   an   the

10. Wow, what _____ hungry duck that is!   a   the

McGraw-Hill Language Arts
10 **Grade 3, Unit 6, Adjectives and Adverbs,**
pages 410–411

At Home: Play a game of "I Spy" with a family member.
Take turns writing sentences that begin with "I spy (a, an,
the) . . ." Use the correct article before each noun.

81

Adverbs

> ### RULES
> - An **adverb** is a word that tells more about a verb.
> - Adverbs tell **how, when,** and **where** an action takes place.
>   *The train moves **swiftly**.* → how
>   *Grandma arrives **tomorrow**.* → when
>   *I see the train **there**.* → where

Circle the adverb that tells about the underlined verb.

1. Dylan's grandmother <u>arrives</u> today.

2. Her train <u>will come</u> soon.

3. Dad <u>parks</u> the car nearby.

4. They <u>go</u> inside.

5. A woman kindly <u>answers</u> their questions.

6. Dylan <u>looks</u> around.

7. Many travelers <u>sit</u> quietly.

8. Some people <u>wait</u> anxiously.

9. Dad and Dylan <u>walk</u> outside.

10. Dylan <u>looks</u> down.

11. Dad <u>listens</u> carefully.

12. The train <u>will arrive</u> early.

13. The train slowly <u>stops</u>.

14. Dylan <u>sees</u> Grandma ahead.

15. He eagerly <u>waves</u> to her.

McGraw-Hill School Division

At Home: With family members, act out meeting someone at a train station. What adverbs describe how you act?

82

McGraw-Hill Language Arts
Grade 3, Unit 6, Adjectives and Adverbs,
pages 412–413

15

Adverbs That Tell *How*

McGraw-Hill School Division

> **RULES**
> - Some **adverbs** tell *how* an action takes place.
> - Adverbs that tell **how** usually end in *-ly*.
>
> The sun shone **bright**⏐ly⏐.   The wind blows **gent**⏐ly⏐.

Circle the adverb that describes the underlined verb. Then, write it on the line.

1. The woods quietly <u>wait</u> for us. _____

2. Deena and I eagerly <u>enter</u> the woods. _____

3. Someone clearly <u>marked</u> a path. _____

4. We easily <u>follow</u> the path. _____

5. We <u>explore</u> curiously. _____

6. Birds <u>sing</u> sweetly. _____

7. The brook <u>flows</u> smoothly. _____

8. Suddenly, a bird <u>flies</u>. _____

9. Its wings <u>flap</u> loudly. _____

10. Deena anxiously <u>looks</u> at me. _____

11. Deena <u>grabs</u> my hand tightly. _____

12. She quickly <u>becomes</u> frightened. _____

13. I <u>whisper</u> softly to her. _____

14. I calmly <u>explain</u> what it was. _____

15. We happily <u>go</u> home. _____

15 **McGraw-Hill Language Arts**
Grade 3, Unit 6, Adjectives and Adverbs,
pages 414–415

At Home: Listen to sounds around you with a family member. Use adverbs to describe the sounds you hear.

83

Adverbs That Tell *When* or *Where*

┌─ **RULES** ───┐

• Some **adverbs** tell **when** or **where** an action takes place.

We wake up [***early***] .   *We drive* [***far***] .

       ↑   ↑

   tells when   tells where

Here are some adverbs that tell **when** and **where.**

When		**Where**	
always	*next*	*ahead*	*here*
early	*soon*	*around*	*outside*
first	*then*	*away*	*there*
later	*today*	*far*	*up*

└───┘

Write **when** or **where** on the line to show what each underlined
adverb tells.

1. <u>Today</u>, we go to the beach.   _____

2. We go <u>there</u> every year.   _____

3. We leave home <u>early</u>.   _____

4. <u>First</u>, we travel for an hour.   _____

5. We <u>always</u> eat a picnic breakfast.   _____

6. We stop <u>here</u> to eat.   _____

7. <u>Then</u>, we drive again.   _____

8. I turn to the car window and look <u>out</u>.   _____

9. Ned looks <u>around</u>, too.   _____

10. <u>Soon</u>, Ned sees the ocean!   _____

11. Ned rushes to the water <u>first</u>.   _____

12. Mom and I join him <u>there</u>.   _____

13. <u>Later</u>, we walk down the beach.   _____

14. We see shells <u>everywhere</u>.   _____

15. It is wonderful <u>here</u>.   _____

At Home: Where does your family like to go together? Take
turns writing about one favorite place. Use adverbs that tell
when and *where.*

McGraw-Hill Language Arts
Grade 3, Unit 6, Adjectives and Adverbs,
pages 416–417

84

15

McGraw-Hill School Division

Combining Sentences: Adjectives and Adverbs

┌─ **RULES** ───┐

• Two sentences that tell about the same person, place, or thing can be **combined by adding an adjective** from one sentence to the other sentence.

    *I'm going to a **party**.*
    *It is a **surprise**.* → *I'm going to a **surprise party**.*

• Two sentences that tell about the same action can be **combined by adding an adverb** from one sentence to the other sentence.

    I'm going to a party.
    *The party is **tomorrow**.* → *I'm going to a party **tomorrow**.*

└───┘

Combine each pair of sentences. Add an adjective or adverb to one of the sentences. Write the new sentence. The first part of each combined sentence is written for you.

1. I wrapped a present. I wrapped it yesterday.

   I wrapped _____

2. The kitten found my present. My present was colorful.

   The kitten _____

3. She tore the wrapping paper. The wrapping paper was pretty.

   She tore _____

4. I found a paper bag. The paper bag was big.

   I found _____

5. I hid the present in the bag. I hid the present today.

   I hid _____

McGraw-Hill Language Arts
Grade 3, Unit 6, Adjectives and Adverbs,
pages 418–419

5

At Home: Show a family member the picture of the kitten tearing the wrapping paper. Write two sentences about the kitten. Use adjectives or adverbs to combine the sentences.

85

Mechanics and Usage: Quotation Marks

┌─ **RULES** ─────────────────────────────────┐
- Use **quotation marks (" ")** to show that someone is speaking.
- Quotation marks come at the beginning and end of a person's exact words.

    "Where are you, Don?" Andrea called.

    "It's time to leave," she said.
└──┘

The underlined words in each sentence show the words someone says. Write out the sentences with the quotation marks added in the correct place.

1. <u>Hurry up,</u> Andrea said to Don.

   _____

2. <u>I'm coming,</u> Don answered.

   _____

3. <u>But I can't find my bus pass,</u> he added.

   _____

4. Andrea said, <u>I will help you look for it.</u>

   _____

5. <u>I've looked everywhere,</u> Don replied.

   _____

6. <u>When did you last see it?</u> Andrea asked.

   _____

7. Don explained, <u>I used it yesterday.</u>

   _____

8. <u>Look in your jacket pocket,</u> Andrea said.

   _____

9. <u>It's there!</u> Don shouted.

   _____

10. He said, <u>I looked everywhere but my pocket.</u>

    _____

At Home: Listen to two family members talking. Write down what they say. Show your family how to add **86** quotation marks where they belong.

McGraw-Hill Language Arts Grade 3, Unit 6, Adjectives and Adverbs, pages 420–421   10

Mixed Review

```
┌─ RULES ────────────────────────────────────────────────┐
│  • An adverb tells more about a verb.                   │
│                                                         │
│  • Adverbs that tell how often end with -ly.            │
│              (sudden + -ly)                             │
│     Dad woke up suddenly.                               │
│                                                         │
│  • Some adverbs tell where or when an action takes place.│
│              (where)                                    │
│     He stood and looked around.                         │
│     (when)                                              │
│     Then he walked into the hallway.                    │
└─────────────────────────────────────────────────────────┘
```

Draw a line under each verb. Then use an adverb from the box to complete each sentence.

swiftly	soon	loudly	eagerly
nearby	peacefully	rapidly	outside
immediately	quickly		

1. Dad listened _____ for the sound.

2. _____ I awoke, too.

3. Heavy footsteps approached _____.

4. They tapped _____ across the porch.

5. Dad lit the porch light _____.

6. We both looked _____.

7. Dad _____ opened the door.

8. Something ran _____ off the porch.

9. We saw the neighbor's dog Thunder _____.

10. We slept _____ the rest of the night.

McGraw-Hill Language Arts
Grade 3, Unit 6, Adjectives and Adverbs,
pages 422–423

At Home: Play What Sound Is It? One person makes a sound in another room and the other person guesses what it is. Use adverbs to help describe the sound.

10

87

Common Errors with Adjectives

> ## RULES
>
> Follow these rules when comparing **two** nouns:
>
> - When the adjective is short, like *green,* add **-er.**
>
>   *Mr. Chang's lawn is **greener** than our lawn.*
> - When the adjective is long, like *comfortable,* use *more* with the adjective.
>
>   *This chair is **more comfortable** than that chair.*
>
> Follow these rules when comparing **more than two:**
>
> - When the adjective is short, like *kind,* add **-est.**
>
>   *Mrs. Thomas is the **kindest** person I know.*
> - When the adjective is long, like *interesting,* use **most** with the adjective.
>
>   *This book is the **most interesting** book I've read.*

Read each sentence. Circle each adjective that compares.

1. Today is the hottest day of the year.

2. The temperature is higher than yesterday.

3. The temperature seems cooler at the beach than at our house.

4. The waves are bigger than before.

5. Near the ocean is the most comfortable place to be.

6. The sand looks darker near the water.

7. Your sand castle is more beautiful than mine!

8. This beach is the nicest one I've seen.

9. The air is fresher here than at home.

10. This has been the most relaxing day ever!

At Home: Ask your family to help you write three
sentences describing the weather, using adjectives
that compare.

88

McGraw-Hill Language Arts
Grade 3, Unit 6, Adjectives and Adverbs,
pages 424–425

10

McGraw-Hill School Division

Study Skills: Thesaurus

RULES

- **Synonyms** are words that have the same or almost the same meaning.

    Happy means almost the same as *glad.*
    Hard means almost the same as *difficult.*

- **Antonyms** are words that have opposite meanings.

    Happy means the opposite of *sad.*
    Hard means the opposite of *easy.*

- A **thesaurus** is a book of synonyms and antonyms. It is a place to find the exact word you need to make your meaning clear.

Look at the first word in each row. Circle the synonym for that word in the row. Then find the antonym in the row. Write it on the line.

1. **large**   big   tiny   middle   far

   _____

2. **bright**   sweet   dull   beautiful   shiny

   _____

3. **neat**   tidy   inquire   messy   new

   _____

4. **scared**   brave   calm   afraid   angry

   _____

5. **fast**   quick   far   slow   late

   _____

McGraw-Hill Language Arts
Grade 3, Unit 6, Study Skills,
pages 432–433

5

At Home: Play a synonym/antonym game. Make 20 word cards. Take turns drawing a card. Write a synonym or antonym on it. The first one to complete 10 cards wins.

89

Vocabulary: Synonyms and Antonyms

- **Synonyms** are words that have the same or almost the same meaning.

    near / close   big / large   begin / start

- **Antonyms** are words that have opposite meanings.

    up / down   hot / cold   high / low

A. Choose a synonym from the box to replace each underlined word. Write the word on the line.

silky bend huge
beautiful strolls

1. My dog is a <u>handsome</u> animal.

   _____

2. His <u>large</u> brown eyes are friendly.

   _____

3. He has a <u>smooth</u> coat.

   _____

4. We like to go for <u>walks</u>.

   _____

5. People <u>lean</u> over to pet my dog.

   _____

B. Choose an antonym from the box to replace each underlined word. Write the word on the line.

sits warm quiet
close thick

6. My cat is a <u>noisy</u> creature. _____

7. She <u>stands</u> in my lap for hours. _____

8. Her <u>thin</u> fur feels soft and silky. _____

9. When I stroke her head, her eyes <u>open</u> happily. _____

10. My cat is a <u>cold</u> friend. _____

At Home: Play a Synonym/Antonym game with family members. Write down a list of words. Say each one aloud and let family members call out a synonym or antonym for it.

90

McGraw-Hill Language Arts
Grade 3, Unit 6, Vocabulary,
pages 434–435

`10`

Composition: Beginning, Middle, End

All good stories have three parts:
- The **beginning** tells who and what the story is about and where and when it takes place.
- The **middle** tells the events, actions, and problems in a story.
- The **end** tells how the story comes out in a way that makes sense.

The beginning tells who or what we will read about. →
(Johnny Appleseed spent his life going around the country planting apple trees.)

The middle tells what happens. ↗
He got the seeds from cider mills. Johnny Appleseed gave the seeds to settlers. He wanted everyone to have apples.

The ending lets us know the story is finished. →
(We can thank Johnny Appleseed for many of our apple trees.)

Circle **beginning** or **end** to tell where each pair of sentences would go in a story.

1. Stormy was the fastest horse in the county. (beginning) end

2. And that's what happened to a horse named Stormy. beginning (end)

3. The girl turned out to be the best trumpet teacher in the state of Texas! beginning (end)

4. Once there was a girl who wanted to play the trumpet. (beginning) end

5. No one ever heard from Sailor Sam again. beginning (end)

6. Have you heard the story of Sailor Sam? (beginning) end

7. Long ago, there was a little house in the big city. (beginning) end

8. The little house was never lonely again. beginning (end)

9. Years later, we published the book and sold 100 copies! beginning (end)

10. One day, Dad and I wrote a book about fishing. (beginning) end

McGraw-Hill Language Arts
Grade 3, Unit 6, Composition,
pages 436–437

10

At Home: Read a favorite story with your family. Find the beginning, middle, and end of the story. Can you think of another end for the story?

91

Sentences

RULES

- A **sentence** is a group of words that tells a complete thought.

  This is a sentence: *We visit the pet store.*

- A **sentence fragment** is a group of words that does not tell a complete thought.

  This is not a sentence: *A small brown dog.*

- Every sentence begins with a capital letter.

Circle each group of words that is a sentence.

1. (Five fish swim in a tank.)

2. Two tiny puppies.

3. (The canaries chirp loudly.)

4. The birds.

5. (Three rabbits nibble on leaves.)

6. (A hamster sleeps in a cage.)

7. (One gerbil runs on a wheel.)

8. Fluffy kittens.

9. (A mouse hides in the straw.)

10. Curls into a ball.

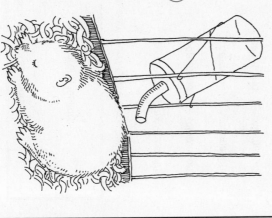

At Home: Draw an animal you would find in a pet store. Work with family members to write three complete sentences about the animal.

Statements and Questions

RULES

- A **statement** is a sentence that tells something.

  The Stamp Museum has exhibits.

- A **question** is a sentence that asks something.

  What kinds of stamps can you see?

- Use a period to end a statement.

- Use a question mark to end a question.

Tell whether the sentence is a statement or a question. Circle the correct word.

1. Stamp collecting is an interesting hobby.   (statement)   question

2. What country is this stamp from?   statement   (question)

3. Tani likes the smallest stamps.   (statement)   question

4. Some stamps are very colorful.   (statement)   question

5. Do you know how old this stamp is?   statement   (question)

6. How much can a rare stamp cost?   statement   (question)

7. Rare stamps can be very expensive.   (statement)   question

8. How many stamps does Tani have?   statement   (question)

9. What is the date on this stamp?   statement   (question)

10. The European stamp exhibit is my favorite.   (statement)   question

At Home: Ask family members to help you collect stamps that come in the mail. Write three statements about the stamps. Then rewrite the statements as questions.

Commands and Exclamations

RULES
- A **command** is a sentence that tells or asks someone to do something.
  Walk carefully in the cave.
- An **exclamation** is a sentence that shows strong feeling.
  Gee, this cave is huge!

Is each sentence a command or an exclamation? Circle the correct word.

1. What a deep cave this is! command (exclamation)

2. Look at the walls. (command) exclamation

3. Don't leave the group. (command) exclamation

4. This cave is very dark! command (exclamation)

5. Wow, these rocks are shiny! command (exclamation)

6. Please walk slowly. (command) exclamation

7. Follow the tour guide. (command) exclamation

8. There are hundreds of bats! command (exclamation)

9. Don't frighten them. (command) exclamation

10. The bats sleep upside down! command (exclamation)

At Home: Choose an outdoor activity that you would like to do with your family. Write five commands about the activity. Then write the commands as exclamations.

□ 10

Mechanics and Usage: Sentence Punctuation

RULES
- End a **statement** and a **command** with a **period**.
  Statement: *The Grand Canyon is made of layers of rock* .
  Command: *Look closely at the different layers* .
- End a **question** with a **question mark**.
  Question: *How many layers can you see* ?
- End an **exclamation** with an **exclamation mark**.
  Exclamation: *Wow, I can see hundreds of layers* !

Circle the correct end punctuation for each sentence.

1. Wow, this is beautiful . ? (!)

2. Why is it called the Grand Canyon . (?) !

3. It is very big and deep (.) ? !

4. Don't get too close to the edge (.) ? !

5. How deep is it . (?) !

6. It is more than a mile deep (.) ? !

7. What a great view this is . ? (!)

8. Aren't you glad we came . (?) !

9. Take some pictures (.) ? !

10. Where is my camera . (?) !

At Home: Find a picture you like of something in nature. Work with a family member to write all four kinds of sentences about the picture.

□ 10

Mixed Review

RULES

- A **sentence** expresses a complete thought. Every sentence begins with a capital letter. A **fragment** does not express a complete thought.
- A **statement** tells something. It ends with a **period.**
  We went sailing on Tuesday.
- A **question** asks something. It ends with a **question mark.**
  Did you have fun?
- A **command** tells or asks someone to do something. It ends with a **period.**
  Tell me what happened.
- An **exclamation** shows strong feeling. It ends with an **exclamation mark.**
  We had a really great day!

For each sentence below, write whether it is a **statement, question, command,** or **exclamation.** Then write the sentence using the correct end mark. Underline any fragments and make them complete sentences.

1. Max went to see the whales
   statement; Max went to see the whales.

2. Where did he go
   question; Where did he go?

3. The big boat
   Possible answer: The big boat sailed away.

4. Don't hang over the rail
   command; Don't hang over the rail.

5. Wow, look at that whale
   exclamation; Wow, look at that whale!

At Home: Invite a family member to ask three questions about whales. Write the questions correctly. Find out the answers, then write them as statements.

5

Subjects in Sentences

RULES

- Every sentence has two parts. The **subject** of a sentence tells what or whom the sentence is about.
  subject → Books
  Books can help us learn.
- The subject of a sentence can be one word or more than one word.
  subject → Many people
  Many people enjoy reading.

Circle the subject in each sentence.

1. The library is a fun place to visit.

2. Hundreds of books sit on the shelves.

3. Adventure books are my favorite.

4. I like to curl up in a corner and read.

5. Some writers are very good at describing things.

6. They paint pictures with words.

7. Science fiction is fun to read, too.

8. Robots and spaceships are interesting.

9. Books about outer space make me want to become an astronaut.

10. I would like to visit another planet.

At Home: With a family member, write three sentences about a favorite story. Point out the subject in each sentence.

6

Predicates in Sentences

RULES

- Every sentence has two parts. The **predicate** of a sentence tells what the subject does or is.

The children **explored the old fort.**

predicate → explored the old fort.

The fort **had huge doors.**

predicate → had huge doors.

Circle the predicate in each sentence.

1. The guide showed the children the fort.

2. The walls are stacked logs.

3. Some of the logs are missing.

4. A high tower stands at that corner.

5. A watchman sat in the tower.

6. He watched for signs of trouble.

7. A small town grew up around the fort.

8. Families of soldiers lived in the fort.

9. The children saw the old schoolroom.

10. The guide took a picture of them.

McGraw-Hill Language Arts
Grade 3, Unit 1, Sentences,
pages 14–15

At Home: Look in a favorite book to find a paragraph about exploring. Share it with a family member. Point out four predicates.

7

10

Combining Sentences: Compound Sentences

RULES

- Two related **sentences can be combined** with a comma and the word and.
- A **compound sentence** is a sentence that contains two sentences joined by and.

Maria has a pet rabbit. It likes to eat lettuce.

Maria has a pet rabbit , **and** it likes to eat lettuce.

Use the word in ( ) to join each pair of sentences.

1. Rabbits are cute. (and) They are also very shy animals.

Rabbits are cute, and they are also very shy animals.

2. They have large ears. (and) They have a good sense of smell.

They have large ears, and they have a good sense of smell.

3. Rabbits feed in the evening. (and) They are always alert.

Rabbits feed in the evening, and they are always alert.

4. Rabbits make nice pets. (and) They need lots of care.

Rabbits make nice pets, and they need lots of care.

5. Rabbits eat a lot. (and) They grow fast.

Rabbits eat a lot, and they grow fast.

McGraw-Hill Language Arts
Grade 3, Unit 1, Sentences,
pages 16–17

At Home: Ask family members to listen as you combine two related sentences about an animal. Use the word and.

8

5

Left page — Reteach 9

Name _____ Date _____ **Reteach** | 9 |

Mechanics and Usage:
Correcting Run-on Sentences

RULES

- A **run-on sentence** joins together two or more sentences.

  The clowns rode on the elephants they waved to the crowd.

- Correct a run-on sentence by separating two ideas into two sentences.

  The clowns rode on the elephants. They waved to the crowd.

- Correct a run-on sentence by writing it as a compound sentence.

  *The clowns rode on the elephants, **and** they waved to the crowd.*

Draw a line between the two sentences. The first one is done for you.

1. The circus has jugglers and tumblers/it has wild animals, too.

2. The circus has horseback riders/they perform tricks.

3. Riders leap on and off a moving horse/they leap through hoops.

4. Clowns are important in the circus/they make people laugh.

5. A traveling circus has a parade/it has wagons and bands.

6. People line the streets to see the parade/the circus performers wave.

7. Bands play marching music/clowns do funny tricks.

8. The circus is held in a tent/it has room for many people.

9. People of all ages go to the circus/they have fun.

10. The circus stays for two weeks/it will be back next year.

McGraw-Hill Language Arts
Grade 3, Unit 1, Sentences,
pages 18-19

| 10 |

At Home: Tell someone in your family what you know
about the circus. Use compound sentences.

9

Right page — Reteach 10

Name _____ Date _____ **Reteach** | 10 |

Mixed Review

RULES

- The **subject** of a sentence tells whom or what the sentence is about.

- The **predicate** of a sentence tells what the subject does or is.

  My family   likes to visit the zoo.
  subject   predicate

- A **compound sentence** contains two related sentences joined by the word *and*.

- A **run-on sentence** contains two or more sentences that should stand alone.

A. Read each sentence. Circle the subject and underline the predicate.

1. (Tigers) have stripes.

2. (The stripes) help the tigers hide.

3. (Tigers) belong to the cat family.

4. (White tigers) are very rare.

5. (Other big cats) include lions and panthers.

B. Read each sentence. Next to each one, write **compound** or **run-on.**

6. Some people see tigers at the zoo, and other people see tigers at the circus. _____ compound

7. I took photos of the tigers, and Jack sketched the lions. _____ compound

8. A trainer can teach a tiger to jump through a hoop sometimes the hoop is on fire. _____ run-on

9. The roar of a tiger is very loud it is scary. _____ run-on

10. Lions roar loudly in the jungle, and the other animals run away. _____ compound

McGraw-Hill Language Arts
Grade 3, Unit 1, Sentences,
pages 20-21

| 10 |

At Home: With a family member, write sentences about other animals in the cat family. Circle the subjects and underline the predicates.

10

McGraw-Hill School Division

T5

Common Errors with Fragments and Run-on Sentences

RULES

- A **sentence fragment** does <u>not</u> express a complete thought. This is a sentence fragment: *Was howling.*
- You can often correct a sentence fragment by adding a subject or a predicate.
- A **run-on sentence** contains two or more sentences that should stand alone.
  This is a run-on sentence: *It is raining we are getting wet.*
- You can correct a run-on sentence by writing it as **two sentences,** or as a **compound sentence.**
  Here are two separate sentences: *It is raining. We are getting wet.*
  Here is a compound sentence: *It is raining, and we are getting wet.*

Write **sentence, fragment,** or **run-on sentence** after each group of words.

1. The weather forecaster. _____ fragment

2. There is a storm approaching the coast. _____ sentence

3. A bad one. _____ fragment

4. Should get. _____ fragment

5. Stay tuned to this station for updates. _____ sentence

6. The next day was sunny and clear trees and other debris covered the ground. _____ run-on sentence

7. A group of volunteers came by to help us clean up the Coast Guard went up and down the coast. _____ run-on sentence

8. Was very lucky. _____ fragment

9. Now our neighborhood is clean again. _____ sentence

10. We have a new club we talk about ways to keep our neighborhood safe during a storm. _____ run-on sentence

McGraw-Hill Language Arts
Grade 3, Unit 1, Sentences,
pages 22–23

10

At Home: Get a copy of your favorite book. Read a paragraph aloud to a family member. Point out the subject and predicate in at least four sentences.

11

Study Skills: Dictionary

RULES

- You use a **dictionary** to find the meanings of words. A dictionary also shows you how words are spelled.
- **Guide words** show the first and last words on a page. They help you locate the entry word.
- **Entry words** are all the words explained in a dictionary. They are listed in ABC order.

Number the words in each list to show the correct ABC order.

1. hut	2	3. junk	3
guide	1	jade	1
icicle	3	jellyfish	2
2. track	3	4. rough	2
skunk	2	rung	3
skate	1	ranch	1

Read each pair of guide words. Circle the word that you would find on a dictionary page with those guide words.

5. march/mattress   (margin)   next   nose

6. float/flute   table   (flood)   three

7. cement/cinder   echo   (center)   zoo

8. salt/sap   earth   (sample)   cook

9. anger/apple   zero   (appeal)   gate

10. pin/pioneer   comb   (pink)   gear

McGraw-Hill Language Arts
Grade 3, Unit 1, Study Skills,
pages 30–31

At Home: Ask a family member to list three words. You put them in ABC order. Have the family member check to make sure you are correct.

12

10

Vocabulary: Time-Order Words

- A time-order word or phrase tells when things happen and in what order.

Before we left on our fishing trip, we ate cereal.

Next, we packed a picnic lunch.

first	second	afterward
next	finally	before
then	third	a long time

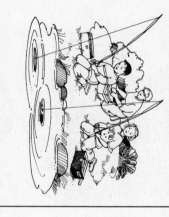

Read each sentence. Write on the line the word or words that show time-order.

1. Fishing can be fun, but first you have to know what to do.

   first

2. You need a good fishing rod before anything else.

   before

3. After you get the rod, practice casting at home in the yard.

   After

4. While you are practicing, ask a friend to dig up some worms.

   While

5. Next, learn how to put the worm on the hook.

   Next

6. You are now ready to try to catch a fish!

   now

7. You might have to sit a long time without getting a bite.

   a long time

8. A fish might not immediately grab the worm.

   immediately

9. A fish may tug on the worm to tease you first.

   first

10. Finally, the fish will grab the worm, and you will catch it!

    Finally

10

At Home: Write directions for making a peanut butter sandwich. Use time-order words like *first, second, next,* and *finally.* Ask a family member to follow your directions.

13

Composition: Main Idea and Supporting Details

- The **main idea** tells what a piece of writing is all about.
- In a good **paragraph**, all sentences should work together to tell about one main idea.
- The main idea of a paragraph is usually told in a **topic sentence.**
- **Supporting details** help to develop and support the main idea.
- If a detail has nothing important to say about the main idea, take it out.
- You can use **time-order words** such as *first, next,* and *before* to connect your ideas.

Read each group of sentences. Find the sentence that tells the main idea and underline it.

1. First, my father spread a blanket on the grass. Then we ate chicken and salad. We spent Saturday afternoon at a family picnic.

2. My sister and I jumped right in. We swam to the raft. We had fun swimming in the lake.

3. My cousins played softball in the field nearby. Marcus hit a home run! Ruthie is the best pitcher.

4. My mother and aunt brought sandwiches. There was so much wonderful food. There was a basket of apples and pears.

5. We flew kites. We played tag. Everyone enjoyed our day in the park.

5

At Home: Find a newspaper article and share it with a family member. Point out the main idea and two supporting details in the article.

14

Nouns

RULES

- A **noun** is a word that names a person, place, or thing.

a person → *boy, woman, worker*
a place → *pool, field, yard*
a thing → *milk, ball, stone*

The **beekeeper** lives nearby. → Beekeeper is a **person**.
He works in his **yard**. → Yard is a **place**.
He gathers **honey**. → Honey is a **thing**.
The words **beekeeper, yard,** and **honey** are all nouns.

Circle the noun in each sentence.

1. There are many (hives) here.

2. (Bees) fly all around.

3. They collect (pollen).

4. They won't sting the (beekeeper).

5. He wears special (clothes).

6. He shows us a (honeycomb).

7. It is made of (wax).

8. There are (cells) in it.

9. This is how they make (honey).

10. We keep it in (jars).

McGraw-Hill Language Arts
Grade 3, Unit 2, Nouns,
pages 78–79

At Home: With a family member, brainstorm nouns about
bees. Draw some cells like a honeycomb in which to write
your nouns.

15

10

Singular and Plural Nouns

RULES

- A **singular noun** names one person, place, or thing.
  person, place, or thing → *boy, school, book*

- A **plural noun** names more than one person, place, or thing.
  persons, places, or things → *boys, schools, books*

- Add **-s** to form the plural of most singular nouns.
  cat + s = cats   *girl + s = girls*

- Add **-es** to form the plural of nouns that end in **s, sh, ch,** or **x.**
  inch + es = inches   *brush + es = brushes*
  dress + es = dresses   *fox + es = foxes*

Read each item on the School Fix-It List. Decide if the underlined
noun is singular or plural. Write **singular** or **plural** on the line.

School Fix-It List

1. Check <u>tires</u> on school <u>bus</u>.   singular

2. Trim <u>bushes</u> near door.   plural

3. Paint bike <u>rack</u>.   singular

4. Replace <u>glass</u> in gym <u>windows</u>.   plural

5. Check <u>light</u> in hallway.   singular

6. Rake <u>leaves</u> on playground.   plural

7. Paint front <u>office</u>.   singular

8. Put empty <u>boxes</u> in trash bin.   plural

9. Repair school <u>clock</u>.   singular

10. Get new <u>cups</u> for office.   plural

McGraw-Hill Language Arts
Grade 3, Unit 2, Nouns,
pages 80–81

At Home: With a family member, make a Fix-It List of your
own. Tell about toys, sports equipment, clothes, or pets that
you need to take care of. Use singular and plural nouns.

16

10

Plural Nouns with -ies

RULES

- If a noun ends in a consonant and the letter *y*, change the *y* to *i* and add **-es** to form the **plural**.

cherry → cherries

I tasted one **cherry.** ← singular

She tasted three **cherries.** ← plural

Write the plural form of each noun in the list.

1. country
   countries

2. guppy
   guppies

3. ferry
   ferries

4. daisy
   daisies

5. grocery
   groceries

6. secretary
   secretaries

7. baby
   babies

8. story
   stories

9. puppy
   puppies

10. family
    families

10

At Home: Draw a picture of a farm, showing ponies, bunnies, and puppies. Label the animals. Show your picture to a family member. Tell how to spell the plural forms.

17

More Plural Nouns

RULES

- Some nouns have special plural forms.

Singular	Plural
One man	Two men
One woman	Three women
One tooth	Four teeth
One mouse	Five mice
One child	Six children

- A few nouns have the same singular and plural forms.

Singular	Plural
One sheep	Two sheep
One deer	Three deer
One moose	Four moose
One fish	Five fish
One trout	Six trout

Write the plural form for each noun.

1. child _____ children

2. tooth _____ teeth

3. deer _____ deer

4. moose _____ moose

5. sheep _____ sheep

6. man _____ men

7. fish _____ fish

8. mouse _____ mice

9. trout _____ trout

10. woman _____ women

10

At Home: Look for a book in the library about sheep, deer, geese, or moose. Share it with a family member. Share what you have learned about singular and plural nouns.

18

Name _____ Date _____

Common and Proper Nouns

RULES

There are two kinds of nouns, common nouns and proper nouns.

- **A common noun** names **any** person, place, or thing. It begins with a small letter.

- **A proper noun** names a **special** person, place, or thing. It can have more than one word. Each important word in a proper noun begins with a capital letter.

a friend	Heather Martin
a city	Los Angeles
a day	Thursday
a river	the Mississippi River

Underline each common noun.
Circle each proper noun.

1. (Lindhurst)

2. (Friday)

3. (Lake Shore Drive)

4. river

5. building

6. doctor

7. (Mary Lee)

8. (Rocky Mountains)

9. (New Jersey)

10. park

At Home: Look at a book of maps with a member of your family. Find names of cities, countries, and bodies of water. Tell why these names begin with capital letters.

Name _____ Date _____

Mechanics and Usage: Capitalization

RULES

- **Capitalize** each important word of a **proper noun**.
- The name of a **day, month,** or **holiday** begins with a capital letter.

Tuesday	July	President's Day

- Words in titles of books begin with capital letters.

Nate's Treasure	Ali Baba and the Forty Thieves

- Do not capitalize a word like *of, the,* and *in* unless it is the first word of a book title.

Read each sentence. Write the underlined proper noun correctly.

1. Geraldo got a new book on <u>monday</u>. _____ Monday

2. The title of the book is <u>nate the great</u>. _____ Nate the Great

3. He will try to finish his book before <u>thanksgiving</u>. _____ Thanksgiving

4. Ravi wants to read <u>eyes of the dragon</u>. _____ Eyes of the Dragon

5. It is about a dragon painter named <u>ch'en jung</u>. _____ Ch'en Jung

6. He will get it at the library on <u>saturday</u>. _____ Saturday

7. The library closes for two weeks in <u>december</u>. _____ December

8. We are joining a book club in <u>january</u>. _____ January

9. The meetings are on <u>wednesday</u> afternoons. _____ Wednesday

10. There is no school on <u>new year's day</u>. _____ New Year's Day

At Home: Ask a family member to name the month in which they were born, a favorite holiday, and favorite book. Write each proper noun correctly.

Mixed Review

RULES

- A **singular noun** names one person, place, or thing.
- A **plural noun** names more than one person, place, or thing.
  - Add **-s** to form most plural nouns: *desk → desks*
  - Add **-es** to form the plural of nouns that end in *s, sh, ch,* or *x*: *lunch → lunches*
  - Some nouns have special plural forms: *mouse → mice*
- A **common noun** names any person, place, or thing.
- A **proper noun** names a special person, place, or thing and begins with a capital letter.
  - Common nouns: *city, holiday, state*
  - Proper nouns: *Chicago, Thanksgiving, Utah*

Read each sentence. Decide if the underlined noun is singular or plural. Then write **singular** or **plural** under it.

1. We had a picnic at the <u>beach</u>.
   singular

2. The <u>sun</u> was shining brightly.
   singular

3. Anya brought the <u>sandwiches</u>.
   plural

4. Did anyone remember to bring <u>dishes</u>?
   plural

5. We ran to put our <u>feet</u> in the water.
   plural

At Home: Look at a magazine or newspaper with a family member. Identify common or proper nouns. Are they singular or plural? See how many you can find.

McGraw-Hill Language Arts
Grade 3, Unit 2, Nouns,
pages 90–91

Singular Possessive Nouns

RULES

- A **possessive noun** shows ownership. It tells who or what owns or has something.
- To form a singular possessive noun, add **'s** to the singular noun.

  singular noun + 's = singular possessive noun

  boy + 's = boy's   *horse + 's = horse's*

  the boy's *coat*   *the* horse's *stall*

Write the possessive noun in each sentence.

1. The art show's theme is "Color in Nature." _____ show's

2. Anna's picture shows a winter scene. _____ Anna's

3. A polar bear's fur blends with the snow. _____ polar bear's

4. Emma's drawing is in the art show, too. _____ Emma's

5. A mouse's dark fur blends with dirt and rocks. _____ mouse's

6. The grasshopper's color blends into the grass. _____ grasshopper's

7. Robert's picture has a jungle setting. _____ Robert's

8. The leopard's spots make the animal hard to see. _____ leopard's

9. The tiger's stripes blend into the shadows. _____ tiger's

10. Nature's paintbox helps many creatures stay safe. _____ Nature's

At Home: Find something in your home that belongs to a family member. Make a sign for it, using a possessive noun.

McGraw-Hill Language Arts
Grade 3, Unit 2, Nouns,
pages 92–93

Plural Possessive Nouns

RULES

- Add an apostrophe (') to make most plural nouns possessive.
  The birds' feathers are beautiful.
- Add an apostrophe (') and an **-s** to form the possessive of plural nouns that do not end in **-s**.
  The children's books are on the shelf.

Write **singular** or **plural** for each underlined possessive noun.

1. the <u>children's</u> faces
   _____ plural

2. the <u>elephants'</u> ears
   _____ plural

3. the <u>monkeys'</u> tails
   _____ plural

4. the <u>bee's</u> sting
   _____ singular

5. the <u>zookeeper's</u> hands
   _____ singular

6. the <u>turtles'</u> tank
   _____ plural

7. the <u>zebra's</u> stripes
   _____ singular

8. the <u>men's</u> cameras
   _____ plural

9. the <u>cage's</u> door
   _____ singular

10. the <u>leopard's</u> spots
    _____ singular

McGraw-Hill Language Arts
Grade 3, Unit 2, Nouns,
pages 94–95

At Home: With a family member, think of people you know who have pets. Write a list of the pets, using possessive nouns: for instance, Tanya's kitten.

Combining Sentences: Nouns

RULES

- You can combine two sentences by joining two nouns.
- **Combining sentences** can make your writing more interesting.
- Use the word **and** to combine the two nouns. Leave out the words that repeat.

> Luis │ built a birdhouse. │
>   ↓
> Kenji │ built a birdhouse. │
>   ↓
> Luis **and** Kenji │ built a birdhouse. │

Read each pair of sentences. Circle the parts that are alike. Then use **and** to combine the sentences.

1. Dean (studied birds.)
   Jan (studied birds.)
   Dean and Jan studied birds.
   _____

2. (They saw) a mother robin.
   (They saw) a father robin.
   They saw a mother robin and a father robin.
   _____

3. (The robins got) straw.
   (The robins got) moss.
   The robins got straw and moss.
   _____

4. (The nest was) soft.
   (The nest was) warm.
   The nest was soft and warm.
   _____

5. Insects (are what robins eat.)
   Worms (are what robins eat.)
   Insects and worms are what robins eat.
   _____

McGraw-Hill Language Arts
Grade 3, Unit 2, Nouns,
pages 96–97

At Home: Write a sentence about what a pet can do. Ask a family member to think of another sentence about that pet. Combine the sentences using and.

Mechanics and Usage: Abbreviations

RULES

- An **abbreviation** is a shortened form of a word.

  Doctor Santos = Dr. Santos

- An abbreviation begins with a capital letter and ends with a period.
- You can abbreviate titles before a name.

  Mrs. Santos   Dr. McCabe   Ms. Gould

- You can abbreviate days of the week.

  Sun.   Mon.   Tues.   Wed.   Thurs.   Fri.   Sat.

- You can abbreviate some months.

  Jan.   Feb.   Mar.   Apr.   Aug.   Sept.   Oct.   Nov.   Dec.

Write whether each underlined abbreviation is a **title**, a **day** of the week, or a **month** of the year.

1. until <u>Sat.</u> _____ day

2. <u>Dr.</u> Cook's friend _____ title

3. by <u>Mon.</u> _____ day

4. beginning of <u>Dec.</u> _____ month

5. early <u>Aug.</u> _____ month

6. with <u>Mr.</u> Reynolds _____ title

7. next <u>Feb.</u> _____ month

8. every <u>Thurs.</u> _____ day

9. <u>Mrs.</u> Riley's class _____ title

10. appointment on <u>Wed.</u> _____ day

McGraw-Hill Language Arts
Grade 3, Unit 2, Nouns,
pages 96–99

At Home: With your family, make a map of your neighborhood. List adults and children in each home. Use abbreviations for titles of people.

25

Mixed Review

RULES

- A possessive **noun** shows who or what owns something.
- Add an apostrophe (') and an **-s** to a singular noun to make it possessive.

  My **sister's** *class went to the zoo.*

- Add an apostrophe to make most plural nouns possessive.

  The **animals'** *keepers brought them food.*

- Add an apostrophe and an **-s** to form the possessive of plural nouns that do not end in **-s.**

  The **children's** *favorite place was the snake house.*

Write the possessive noun from each sentence.

1. The zookeeper's office is by the main entrance. _____ zookeeper's

2. The monkeys' house is near the elephant pen. _____ monkeys'

3. The elephants' keeper is feeding them. _____ elephants'

4. The giraffe's baby is standing near her mother. _____ giraffe's

5. The man's camera is ready. _____ man's

6. The camera's flash is bright. _____ camera's

7. The baby's picture will be in the paper. _____ baby's

8. The picture's quality will be clear. _____ picture's

9. The children's teacher pointed to the monkeys. _____ children's

10. The animals' antics made them laugh. _____ animals'

McGraw-Hill Language Arts
Grade 3, Unit 2, Nouns,
pages 100–101

At Home: Make a list of things you can see at the zoo. With a family member, write five sentences that use possessive nouns. For example, *The monkeys' tails are long.*

26

Common Errors with Plurals and Possessives

RULES

Writers often make mistakes when writing plural nouns and possessive nouns.

- A **plural noun** names more than one person, place, or thing.

  farmers   fields   geese

- A **possessive noun** shows who or what owns or has something.

- To form the possessive of a singular noun, add an **'s**.

  | The | **farmer's** | field is filled with wheat. |

- To form the possessive of a plural noun that ends in -s, add an apostrophe (').

  | The | **farmers'** | fields are filled with wheat. |

- To form the possessive of a plural noun that does not end in -s, add an **'s**.

  | The | **geese's** | eggs are large. |

Read the sentences. Circle the word in ( ) that is the correct plural or possessive noun. Then write it on the line.

1. The (children's, childrens', childrens) teacher took them to a farm.

   children's

2. The (farmers', farmer's, farmers) tractor is red.

   farmer's

3. The (geese, gooses', goose's) feathers are soft.

   goose's

4. The (geese, goose, goose's) live in a big pen.

   geese

5. The (pigs, pigs', pig's) name is Wilbur.

   pig's

At Home: With a family member, think of four animals you might find on a farm. Then write sentences about the animals using plural and possessive nouns.

Study Skills: Library Resources

- The **library** is a good source of information. To locate information in the library, use the **Library Card Catalog** or **PAC (Public Access Catalog)**. In most libraries, the catalog, or PAC, is on the computer.

- The **card catalog** lists all the books and materials in the library. The card catalog contains a **title card** and an **author card** for every book. Each nonfiction book also has a **subject card**. The cards are arranged in alphabetical order.

- Every book has a **call number** that identifies what category of book it is. It can help you find the book on the shelf.

Title Cards	**Author Cards**	**Subject Cards**
↓	↓	↓
If you know the **title** of the book you want, use this card.	If you know the **author** of the book you want, use this card.	If you know the **subject** of the book you want, use this card.

Write what kind of card in the card catalog you would use to find the following information.

1. Books about kangaroos _____ subject card

2. A story about a pretend place by Alice McLerran _____ author card

3. A list of books by Beverly Cleary _____ author card

4. A book called *Ibis: A True Whale Story* _____ title card

5. Books about George Washington _____ subject card

6. A mystery story by Johnny Alcorn _____ author card

7. A book called *The Puffins Are Back* _____ title card

8. A book about a cowboy named Pecos Bill _____ subject card

9. A list of books by Gail Gibbons _____ author card

10. Books about football _____ subject card

At Home: With a family member, choose a subject, author, or title of a book. Then go to the library together and look for the book by using the card catalog.

McGraw-Hill School Division

Vocabulary: Compound Words

A **compound word** is a word made by joining two or more words together.

mail + box   A **mailbox** is a **box for mail.**

paint + brush   A **paintbrush** is a **brush for painting.**

sun + light   **Sunlight** is **light from the sun.**

back + pack   A **backpack** is a **pack you wear on your back.**

Circle the compound word in each pair. Write the two words that make up the compound word on the lines below it.

1. (basketball), berries

basket _____ ball _____

2. (moonlight), mostly

moon _____ light _____

3. notice, (notebook)

note _____ book _____

4. surely, (sunburn)

sun _____ burn _____

5. (halfway), habit

half _____ way _____

6. (haircut), handle

hair _____ cut _____

7. topic, (toothache)

tooth _____ ache _____

8. seat, (seashore)

sea _____ shore _____

9. (windowsill), windy

window _____ sill _____

10. (barefoot), baby

bare _____ foot _____

At Home: Find items in your home with compound word names, such as *toothbrush, washcloth,* and *bathtub.* Make a list of these words and explain it to a family member.

29

Composition: Organization

• Writing about ideas, events, or instructions is like solving a problem. You must present the details in an order that makes sense.

• What are you going to tell about? Begin with a **topic sentence** that tells the main idea.

• What order should you choose? Try to tell things in time order with **step-by-step details.** Keep in mind what is **first, second, third,** and so on.

• How can special words help? Begin your sentences with words such as **First, Next,** and **Last.**

Rewrite the paragraph on the lines below. Draw a line under the topic sentence. Circle each time-order word.

    Follow these easy steps to give your dog a bath. First, put your dog in a tub of warm water. Second, wash your dog all over using baby shampoo. Next, rinse your dog with clean water. Last, dry your dog with thick, dry towels.

Follow these easy steps to give your dog a bath. (First,) put your

dog in a tub of warm water. (Second,) wash your dog all over using

baby shampoo. (Next,) rinse your dog with clean water. (Last,) dry

your dog with thick, dry towels.

_____

_____

_____

_____

_____

_____

At Home: With a family member, make a chart about washing dishes. Tell what to do in 4 or 5 steps. Make sure the steps are in order. Then post your chart on the refrigerator.

30

Name _____ Date _____ **Reteach** 31

Action Verbs

RULES

- An **action verb** is a word that shows action.

  Ariel paints pictures in her free time.

- Some action verbs tell about actions that we cannot see.

  Ariel believes her brother.

- In a sentence, the subject does some action. The action verb answers the question, "What does the subject do?"

  Tim washes the paintbrushes.

  What does Tim do?

  Tim washes the paintbrushes.

Read each sentence. Ask what the subject does. Find the words that show action. Circle each action verb.

1. Miike (goes) to his art class.

2. The students (button) their smocks.

3. The students (mold) the clay.

4. Miike (creates) a clay pot.

5. The teacher (takes) the pot to the kiln.

6. Artists (work) with different materials.

7. Potters (use) clay, a potter's wheel, and a kiln.

8. A potter's wheel (turns) very quickly.

9. The artists (make) pottery of many shapes and sizes.

10. Later, everyone (paints) the pottery.

 10

McGraw-Hill Language Arts
Grade 3, Unit 3, Verbs,
pages 160–161

At Home: Use action words to tell your family what you did at school today.

31

McGraw-Hill School Division

Name _____ Date _____ **Reteach** 32

Present-Tense Verbs

RULES

- The **tense** of a verb tells when the action takes place.
- Verbs in the **present tense** tell what happens now.
- Follow these rules when you use present-tense verbs with singular subjects.
- Add **-s** to most singular verbs in → *Miss Muffet sits down.* the present tense.
- Add **-es** to verbs that end in *sh*, → *The spider watches Miss Muffet.* *ch*, *ss*, *s*, *zz*, or *x*.
- Change *y* to *i* and add **-es** to → *Miss Muffet cries for help.* verbs that end in a consonant and a *y* together.

Circle the verb in ( ) that has the correct spelling.

1. The gingerbread man (runes, (runs)) away.

2. The fox (carrys, (carries)) him through the water.

3. Everyone (chases, chasies) after him.

4. Mama Bear (fixes, fixs) porridge.

5. Goldilocks (gets, getes) lost in the woods.

6. Baby Bear (watchs, (watches)) the girl sleep.

7. Gepetto (wishs, (wishes)) on a star.

8. Pinocchio (trys, (tries)) to be an actor.

9. Gepetto (misses, misss) Pinocchio.

10. Pinocchio (changes, changies) into a donkey.

32

McGraw-Hill Language Arts
Grade 3, Unit 3, Verbs,
pages 162–163

At Home: Draw pictures of a favorite storybook character doing something. Tell a family member about the character, using present-tense verbs.

10

T16

Subject-Verb Agreement

RULES

- A **present-tense** verb must agree with its subject.
- Do not add **-s** or **-es** to a present-tense verb when the subject is plural.

  The children need a computer.
  Computers change our lives.

- Do not add **-s** or **-es** to a present-tense verb when the subject is *I* or *you.*

  You use computers for schoolwork.
  I see computers every day.

Write the correct form of the verb in ( ).

1. Computers (give, gives) us information.
   give

2. The information (help, helps) us.
   helps

3. We (know, knows) some things.
   know

4. A student (learn, learns) many new things.
   learns

5. You (find, finds) interesting facts.
   find

6. Many people (buy, buys) computers.
   buy

7. A teacher (load, loads) software into the computer.
   loads

8. I (put, puts) in the disks.
   put

9. You (press, presses) the keys.
   press

10. The keys (give, gives) commands.
    give

 10

McGraw-Hill Language Arts
Grade 3, Unit 3, Verbs,
pages 164–165

At Home: Tell your family how you use or would like to use computers in school. Make sure that you use correct subject-verb agreement.

33

Mechanics and Usage: Letter Punctuation

RULES

- Use a capital letter for the first word and the name in the greeting and the closing of a letter.

  Dear Uncle Peter,
  Love,
  Pat

- Put a comma at the end of the greeting. Put a comma between the closing and the signature.

  Dear Uncle Peter,
  Love,
  Pat

Circle the correct answer in each pair.

1. Dear, Chris | **Dear Chris,**

2. **Sincerely,** | Sincerely
   Clarissa | Clarissa

3. **Yours truly,** | Yours Truly,
   Kevin | Kevin

4. **Dear Mario,** | dear Mario,
   Yuko | Yuko

5. **Your Friend** | Your friend,
   Yuko | Yuko

6. Dear grandpa, | **Dear Grandpa,**

7. Love | **Love,**
   Courtney | Courtney

8. dear Sonia, | **Dear Sonia,**

9. **Sincerely yours,** | Sincerely Yours,
   Stephen | Stephen

10. **Dear Jada,** | Dear Jada

Jan. 1, 2004

Dear Gina,
I had fun. Hope you
can come to my house
again soon.
Your friend,
Susan

10

McGraw-Hill Language Arts
Grade 3, Unit 3, Verbs,
pages 166–167

At Home: Write a letter with a family member. Take turns thinking of greetings and closings. Then choose the greeting and closing that are most appropriate.

34

Mixed Review

RULES

- An **action verb** shows action.
- Add **-s** or **-es** to most singular verbs in the present tense. If a verb ends with a consonant and **y**, change the **y** to **i** and add **-es**.

My teacher | takes | us to the Sky Dome.

My class | studies | astronomy.

- If the subject of a sentence is plural or is **I**, **you**, or **we**, do not add -s or -es to the verb in the present tense.

We | look | through a telescope.

I | find | a star right away.

Read each sentence. Write the correct form of the verb in ( ) on the line.

1. We (watch, watches) the stars in the Sky Dome. ___ watch

2. I (explore, explores) the night sky with a big telescope. ___ explore

3. Tim (look, looks) at the stars. ___ looks

4. He (see, sees) many stars and planets. ___ sees

5. Our planet (move, moves) in space. ___ moves

6. The planets (circle, circles) the sun. ___ circle

7. Astronomers (work, works) when it's dark. ___ work

8. An astronomer (study, studies) the position of the stars. ___ studies

9. A new star (appear, appears) suddenly in the sky. ___ appears

10. Astronomers (take, takes) photos of these events. ___ take

 10

At Home: Watch a sports event with a family member. Describe the event. Be sure to use colorful action verbs to describe what you see. Use the correct verb forms.

Past-Tense Verbs

RULES

- A **past-tense verb** tells about an action that happened already. Add **-ed** to most verbs to form the past tense.

We **visited** a science museum last week.

- When adding the **-ed** ending, some verbs change their spelling.
- For verbs that end with a consonant and **y**: Change the **y** to **i** before adding **-ed**.

try → **tried**   spy → **spied**

- For verbs that end in **e**: Drop the **e** and add **-ed**.

close → **closed**   bake → **baked**

- For verbs that end with one vowel and one consonant: Double the consonant and add **-ed**.

hug → **hugged**   pat → **patted**

Underline the past-tense verb in each sentence.

1. We explored the museum.

2. We stopped at every exhibit.

3. They showed us a lot about inventions.

4. The signs explained the inventions.

5. Inventions changed our lives.

6. We watched a movie about Thomas Edison.

7. It showed his invention of the light bulb.

8. I liked it a lot.

9. Then we shopped at the museum store.

10. We hurried back to the school bus just in time.

10

At Home: Talk with your family about what you learned or might have learned on a trip to a museum. Use past-tense verbs.

McGraw-Hill School Division

T18

Future-Tense Verbs

RULES

- A **future-tense verb** tells about an action that is going to happen. Use **will** with the action verb to tell about the future.

  *Tomorrow we **will go** on a field trip.*

  *I **will have** a great time.*

  Present Tense → The show starts.

  Past Tense → The show started.

  Future Tense → The show **will start.**

Underline the verb in each sentence. Then circle *present, past,* or *future* to tell the tense.

1. Our class will take a trip to the theater.   present   past   (future)

2. We will watch a play.   present   past   (future)

3. We visited the theater last year.   present   (past)   future

4. The bus leaves early for trips.   (present)   past   future

5. We will see "Sadako and the Thousand Paper Cranes."   present   past   (future)

6. We will wear nice clothes.   present   past   (future)

7. Some students will buy food there.   present   past   (future)

8. Others will bring their own food.   present   past   (future)

9. We will arrive home late.   present   past   (future)

10. Everyone loves these field trips.   (present)   past   future

10
McGraw-Hill Language Arts
Grade 3, Unit 3, Verbs,
pages 172–173

37

At Home: Talk with your family about a trip you would like to take some day and what you will do. Listen for future-tense verbs.

Combining Sentences: Verbs

RULES

- Join two sentences that have the same subject by **combining the predicates.**

  Roxy finds leaves.

  Roxy makes leaf prints.

  Roxy finds leaves and makes leaf prints.

- Use the word **and** to combine the predicates.

  Roxy gets a large crayon.

  Roxy rubs the paper.

  Roxy gets a large crayon **and** ~~Roxy~~ rubs the paper.

Use *and* to combine the predicates of each pair of sentences. Write the new sentence.

1. Our club creates art.
   Our club makes crafts.
   Our club creates art and makes crafts.

2. Ms. Lin shows us ideas.
   Ms. Lin helps us choose one.
   Ms. Lin shows us ideas and helps us choose one.

3. We select our materials.
   We find a place to work.
   We select our materials and find a place to work.

4. Jeff takes the scissors.
   Jeff cuts pieces of felt.
   Jeff takes the scissors and cuts pieces of felt.

5. Robby reads the directions.
   Robby follows them.
   Robby reads the directions and follows them.

38

McGraw-Hill Language Arts
Grade 3, Unit 3, Verbs,
pages 174–175

5

At Home: Tell a family member how you made a craft item or did an art project. Use *and* to combine sentences.

Mechanics and Usage:
Commas in Dates and Places

RULES

- Use a **comma** between the names of a city or town and state.

  Seattle [,] Washington

  Union City [,] New Jersey

- Use a **comma** between the day and the year in a date.

  September 26 [,] 2001

Write the dates and places. Put the comma in the correct place in each.

1. Gary Indiana _____ **Gary, Indiana**

2. January 10 2005 _____ **January 10, 2005**

3. February 26 2004 _____ **February 26, 2004**

4. Carson City Nevada _____ **Carson City, Nevada**

5. Augusta Maine _____ **Augusta, Maine**

6. April 4 1995 _____ **April 4, 1995**

7. Santa Fe New Mexico _____ **Santa Fe, New Mexico**

8. January 11 2010 _____ **January 11, 2010**

9. Eugene Oregon _____ **Eugene, Oregon**

10. December 25 2050 _____ **December 25, 2050**

McGraw-Hill Language Arts
Grade 3, Unit 3, Verbs,
pages 176–177

At Home: Write the birth dates and hometowns of your
family members. Use commas where they belong.

39

Mixed Review

RULES

- Add -ed to most verbs to show action that happened in the past.

Present	Past
I **look** at you.	I **looked** at you.

- Use **will** with action verbs to tell about something
  that is going to happen in the future.

Present	Future
I **look** at you.	I **will look** at you.

- Use the word **and** to join the predicates of two sentences with the
  same subject.

  Marlene's plant is green. Marlene's plant grows quickly.

  Marlene's plant is green **and** grows quickly.

Read each sentence. Write the verb in the tense shown in ( ).

1. Marlene (worry, *past tense*) about her plant. _____ **worried**

2. Her father (want, *past tense*) to move it. _____ **wanted**

3. "Your plant (grow, *future tense*) better near the light," he said. _____ **will grow**

4. Marlene (lift, *past tense*) her flowerpot. _____ **lifted**

5. She (place, *past tense*) it on the windowsill. _____ **placed**

6. The sun (shine, *future tense*) on it in the afternoon. _____ **will shine**

7. The plant (need, *future tense*) water. _____ **will need**

8. She (sprinkle, *future tense*) it with water. _____ **will sprinkle**

9. "I (give, *future tense*) it some plant food, too," she said. _____ **will give**

10. Marlene's plant (improve, *future tense*) now. _____ **will improve**

McGraw-Hill Language Arts
Grade 3, Unit 3, Verbs,
pages 178–179

At Home: With a family member, make a "Past and Future"
chart. On one side, write sentences with past-tense verbs.
On the other, write sentences with future-tense verbs.

40

Common Errors with Subject-Verb Agreement

RULES

The **subject** and **verb** in a sentence must always agree.

- If the subject is one person or thing, then the verb must tell about one person or thing. Add -s or -es to the verb.

  This sentence is _not_ correct: My brother **pack** for the trip.
  This sentence is correct: My brother **packs** for the trip.

- If the subject is more than one person or thing, then the verb must tell about more than one person or thing.

  This sentence is _not_ correct: His friends **watch.**
  This sentence is correct: His friends **watches.**

- If the subject has two nouns joined by _and,_ then the verb must tell about two subjects.

  This sentence is _not_ correct: Mom and I **helps.**
  This sentence is correct: Mom and I **help.**

Read each sentence. Circle the verb in ( ) that agrees with the subject.

1. This spacecraft (takes, take) us to the moon.

2. The spacecraft (carries, carry) us there in just three days.

3. Our pilot (flies, fly) at top speed.

4. We (hopes, hope) to see a view of Earth.

5. I (loves, love) my home on the moon.

6. Our family (lives, live) in a domed city.

7. Dad's robot (meets, meet) us at the Moon Dock.

8. Mom (wants, want) news from her friends on Earth.

9. Our cousins (plans, plan) to visit us for the holidays.

10. My brother and I (see, sees) the Earth from our window!

10

At Home: Think of a place you want to go. Write a story about it. Make sure the subjects and verbs agree, then point them out to a family member.

41

Study Skills: Note-Taking and Summarizing

RULES

- One way to remember what you read is to **take notes** about the main idea and details.

- Then you can write a **summary** to state briefly the main idea and the important details.

Read the summary. Follow the directions to write the main idea and the important facts.

Cheetahs hunt differently from other big cats. Most big cats hunt at night. They hide themselves, wait for their prey, and then leap out. Cheetahs hunt in broad daylight. When they spot their prey, they come out in the open. When their prey starts to run, cheetahs chase them at top speed. If cheetahs have to run longer than a minute, they give up and go away.

1. Write the main-idea sentence.
   Cheetahs hunt differently from other big cats.

2. Write a sentence that tells a fact about when most big cats hunt.
   Most big cats hunt at night.

3. Write a sentence that tells an important fact about how most big cats hunt. They hide themselves, wait for their prey, and then leap out.

4. Write a sentence that tells an important fact about when cheetahs hunt.
   Cheetahs hunt in broad daylight.

5. Write a sentence that tells an important fact about how cheetahs hunt.
   When they spot their prey, they come out in the open. (or)
   When their prey starts to run, cheetahs chase them at top speed.
   (or) If cheetahs have to run longer than a minute, they give up and go away.

5

At Home: Find a book about an animal. With a family member, choose an interesting paragraph. Decide which sentence is the main idea. Choose another sentence that tells an important fact.

42

McGraw-Hill School Division

T21

Vocabulary: Prefixes

• A **prefix** is a word part that is added to the beginning of a word. It changes the meaning of the base word.

Prefix	Meaning		Example	
dis- =	opposite of	→	**dis** + connect	- disconnect
dis- =	not	→	**dis** + honest	- dishonest
re- =	again	→	**re** + enter	- reenter
un- =	not	→	**un** + able	- unable
un- =	opposite of	→	**un** + cover	- uncover

Circle the word in each row that has a prefix.

1. (unlike)   universe   unless
2. disk   (distaste)   different
3. usable   (unwrap)   umbrella
4. radish   radio   (review)
5. (distrust)   desert   deserve
6. (reword)   reason   really
7. unit   ugly   (unchain)
8. dipper   drink   (disorder)
9. (resend)   read   reptile
10. uncle   utter   (unreal)

At Home: With a family member, look at advertisements in an old magazine. Find as many words as you can with the prefixes *dis-*, *re-*, and *un-*. Cut them out and make a word collage.

Composition: Leads and Endings

A good **lead:**
• gets the readers' attention and makes them want to read more.
• may give the main idea.

A good **ending:**
• lets the readers know that the story is finished.
• may draw a conclusion, state the main idea again, or sum up what the writer said.

Read each sentence. Write on the line if it is a **lead** or an **ending**.

1. In closing, I hope you come to my concert. _____ ending

2. Our new park has opened, and it's fun, fun, fun! _____ lead

3. Have you ever seen wild wolves? _____ lead

4. Today I'll tell you about my adventure. _____ lead

5. That was the funniest event in my life. _____ ending

6. Finally, we all got home. _____ ending

7. Guess what you'll see at City Center? _____ lead

8. I am sure I'll never forget that day. _____ ending

9. Learn to sew in three easy steps! _____ lead

10. We have a new member in our family. _____ lead

At Home: Look at some of your favorite storybooks. With a member of your family, read the beginnings and endings of three stories.

Main and Helping Verbs

RULES
- Sometimes a verb may be more than one word.

  has planned   is thinking

- The **main verb** tells what the subject does or is.

  *Our class is **going** on a picnic.*

- The **helping verb** helps the main verb show an action.

  *Our class **is** going on a picnic.*

- Here are some verbs often used as helping verbs.

have	am	was
has	is	were
had	are	will

Circle the main verb and underline the helping verb in each sentence.

1. Everyone has packed a lunch.

2. Mrs. DeWall is bringing a watermelon.

3. Mr. Lopez will plan some games.

4. Miguel and Kurt have brought a baseball.

5. Melissa and Thomas were carrying some water jugs.

6. Thomas had thrown a ball to Luis.

7. Louise was getting a drink of water.

8. I am hiding behind the tree.

9. Pete has fun after a rabbit.

10. Luis and I are running after Pete.

McGraw-Hill Language Arts
Grade 3, Unit 4, Verbs,
pages 240–241

At Home: Ask family members what they like to do on a picnic. Write three sentences about the activities using main and helping verbs.

45

Using Helping Verbs

RULES
- Use the **helping verbs** *has, have,* and *had* to help main verbs show an action in the past.

- Both the main verb and the helping verb must agree with the subject of the sentence.

  *John **has** gone to the library.*

  *Anna and Sue **have** worked on a report.*

  *John **had** taken out two library books.*

Circle the correct helping verb to use in each sentence.

1. My class (have, has) studied insects.

2. I (had, has) written a report about bees.

3. Paul (have, had) written his report about grasshoppers.

4. We (has, have) displayed our reports in the library.

5. Other students (have, has) seen our reports.

6. The bees (have, has) built a hive.

7. A bee (have, has) collected pollen.

8. The queen bee (have, has) laid some eggs.

9. The bees (have, has) made some honey.

10. I (have, has) learned a lot about bees.

McGraw-Hill Language Arts
Grade 3, Unit 4, Verbs,
pages 242–243

At Home: With a family member, choose an animal. Write three sentences about what the animal does. Be sure to use helping verbs with the main verbs.

46

Linking Verbs

Name _____ Date _____ **Reteach** **47**

RULES

- A **linking verb** does not show action. It connects the subject to a noun or an adjective in the predicate.

  The monkey is cute.

- The verb **be** is a common linking verb.

  Raj is at the zoo.

  I am at the zoo, too.

Draw a line under each verb. Write **linking verb** or **action verb** to describe each verb.

1. We looked into the monkey cage. _____ action verb

2. The monkeys were loud. _____ linking verb

3. The littlest monkey was the cutest. _____ linking verb

4. One large monkey swung from a tall tree. _____ action verb

5. He played with another monkey. _____ action verb

6. My baby brother is asleep. _____ linking verb

7. I am tired, too. _____ linking verb

8. Our family leaves the zoo. _____ action verb

9. We walk to our car. _____ action verb

10. The zoo was fun. _____ linking verb

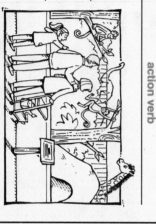

McGraw-Hill Language Arts
Grade 3, Unit 4, Verbs,
pages 244–245

At Home: Talk with your family about a trip you have taken. Write three sentences about it. Underline the action or linking verbs in each sentence.

10

47

Using Linking Verbs

Name _____ Date _____ **Reteach** **48**

RULES

- Use the linking verbs **is, am,** and **was** when the subject of the sentence is singular.

  I am at camp all week.

  My friend Eric is at camp, too.

  Our favorite counselor was at camp last week.

- Use **are** and **were** with a plural subject and **you.**

  Eric and I are at camp all week.

  We were at camp last week, too.

If the correct linking verb is used, write **correct.** If an incorrect linking verb is used, write **incorrect.**

1. Today is field day at camp. _____ correct

2. My friend and I is in two events. _____ incorrect

3. I am in the relay race. _____ correct

4. Trevor and Casey is on the team, too. _____ incorrect

5. We was the winners last year. _____ incorrect

6. Some of the children were on the swim team. _____ correct

7. I was not on the swim team. _____ correct

8. The sun are not warm today. _____ incorrect

9. The lake are very cold. _____ incorrect

10. I am ready for the race. _____ correct

McGraw-Hill Language Arts
Grade 3, Unit 4, Verbs,
pages 246–247

At Home: With a family member, talk about what you did or would like to do on a family trip. Write three sentences about these activities. Use at least one linking verb.

10

48

McGraw-Hill School Division

T24

Mechanics and Usage: Commas in a Series

RULES

- Use **commas** to separate three or more words in a series.
- Do not use a comma after the last word in a series.

  Mom, Dad, and I are going to the circus.

Write each group of words. Add commas where needed.

1. tigers elephants and horses
   tigers, elephants, and horses

2. clowns tightrope walkers and lion tamers
   clowns, tightrope walkers, and lion tamers

3. pizza popcorn and peanuts
   pizza, popcorn, and peanuts

4. bicycles tricycles and unicycles
   bicycles, tricycles, and unicycles

5. lions tigers and elephants
   lions, tigers, and elephants

6. the clowns the dogs and the ponies
   the clowns, the dogs, and the ponies

7. laughed cheered and clapped
   laughed, cheered, and clapped

8. a program some popcorn and a drink
   a program, some popcorn, and a drink

9. a silly hat a balloon and a poster
   a silly hat, a balloon, and a poster

10. My mom my dad my sister and I
    My mom, my dad, my sister, and I

10

McGraw-Hill Language Arts
Grade 3, Unit 4, Verbs,
pages 248–249

At Home: With a family member, choose a special event you attended together. Write a sentence telling three things you liked about the event. Be sure to use commas as needed.

Mixed Review

RULES

- The **main verb** tells what the subject is or does.
- A **helping verb** comes before the main verb. It helps the main verb show action.

  *My family **raises** Great Danes.*

                    helping verb   main verb

  *Mom   **is**   **taking**   the dogs for a walk.*

- Use the helping verbs **has, have,** and **had** to help main verbs show an action in the past.
- The **linking verb be** does not show action.
- Use **is, am,** and **was** with singular subjects.

  *Our oldest dog **is** white with big black spots.*

- Use **are** and **were** with plural subjects and you.

  *The dogs **are** very well trained.*

Read each sentence. Draw a box around the linking verb. Draw a line under a main verb with a helping verb.

1. The big event each year [is] the dog show.

2. We are taking our Great Danes in a van.

3. A trainer is trotting them around the ring.

4. By this time last year, our dog Brutus had won first place.

5. My sister and I are taking turns grooming our dogs.

6. I was brushing Brutus before the show.

7. He is wearing a beautiful silver collar with gold stars on it.

8. Other kinds of dogs [are] at the dog show.

9. This morning I was watching the beagles with their long, floppy ears.

10. The collies [are] always so loud!

10

McGraw-Hill Language Arts
Grade 3, Unit 4, Verbs,
pages 250–251

At Home: With a family member, write five things a dog can do. Use main verbs with helping verbs, linking verbs, and action verbs.

Irregular Verbs

RULES

- An irregular verb has a special spelling to show the past tense.
- Some irregular verbs have a special spelling when used with a helping verb.

Present	Past	With Helping Verbs
come	came	had, has, or have come
do	did	had, has, or have done
say	said	had, has, or have said
go	went	had, has, or have gone
run	ran	had, has, or have run
see	saw	had, has, or have seen
drive	drove	had, has, or have driven

Circle the past tense of each verb in ( ). Then write it on the line.

1. We (go, (went)) to the beach. _____ went

2. We (see, (saw)) lots of shells. _____ saw

3. Two boys ((ran), run) by us. _____ ran

4. We ((said), say) hello to them. _____ said

5. The boys (do, (did)) a double-take. _____ did

6. We ((had seen), see) the boys before. _____ had seen

7. Those boys ((had come), come) last summer. _____ had come

8. They (come, (came)) to the beach with their parents. _____ came

9. We ((had gone), go) fishing with them last year. _____ had gone

10. We (has gone, (went)) fishing in their boat. _____ went

McGraw-Hill Language Arts
Grade 3, Unit 4, Verbs,
pages 252–253

At Home: Ask a family member to tell about a suprise meeting. Write about it, using at least two irregular verbs.

51

More Irregular Verbs

RULES

- **Irregular verbs** do not add **-ed** to show past tense.
- Irregular verbs have special spellings in the past tense and when they are used with a helping verb.

Present	Past	With Helping Verbs
begin	began	had, has, or have begun
eat	ate	had, has, or have eaten
give	gave	had, has, or have given
grow	grew	had, has, or have grown
sing	sang	had, has, or have sung
bring	brought	had, has, or have brought

Circle the irregular verb in each sentence.

1. Grandpa (had given) me a zucchini plant.

2. The zucchini plant has (grown) very large.

3. The zucchini plant has (began) to sprout.

4. I (brought) the zucchinis to my mother.

5. We have (eaten) a lot of zucchinis.

6. I have (sung) to my plant.

7. I have (given) my plant vitamins.

8. My plant has (grown) large.

9. I (brought) some of my zucchinis to a sick friend.

10. I (gave) some seeds to my friend.

McGraw-Hill Language Arts
Grade 3, Unit 4, Verbs,
pages 254–255

At Home: Write some sentences about a plant. Be sure to include at least one irregular verb in your writing. Show your writing to a family member.

Contractions with Not

RULES

- A **contraction** is a shortened form of two words. In a contraction, one or more letters are left out.
- Use an **apostrophe (')** to take the place of the missing letter or letters.

  have not = haven't   is not = isn't
  are not = aren't   was not = wasn't
  cannot = can't   do not = don't
  does not = doesn't   were not = weren't

- The word **won't** is a special contraction. In this contraction, the spelling of **will** changes.

  will not = won't

Look at the words in the first column. Then circle the correct contractions formed from the words.

1. is not   (isn't)   aren't   can't

2. should not   won't   didn't   (shouldn't)

3. will not   wouldn't   (won't)   wasn't

4. were not   (weren't)   wasn't   hadn't

5. had not   hasn't   (hadn't)   haven't

6. are not   (aren't)   can't   couldn't

7. does not   don't   didn't   (doesn't)

8. did not   can't   doesn't   (didn't)

9. has not   (hasn't)   hadn't   haven't

10. was not   (wasn't)   weren't   won't

McGraw-Hill Language Arts
Grade 3, Unit 4, Verbs,
pages 256–257

At Home: With a family member, think of three rules you have in your home. Write these rules using contractions.

10

Combining Sentences: Verbs

RULES

- Two sentences with the **same subject** can be combined.
- Use the word **and** to join the predicates.

Write each pair of sentences as one sentence on the lines below.
Use the word and to combine the predicates.

1. We saw a huge model airplane.
   We walked up close to it.
   We saw a huge model airplane and walked up close to it.

2. A man talked about the Wright brothers.
   A man described the first airplane.
   A man talked about the Wright brothers and described the first airplane.

3. The Wright brothers read many books.
   The Wright brothers did many experiments.
   The Wright brothers read many books and did many experiments.

4. They built an airplane.
   They brought it to Kitty Hawk.
   They built an airplane and brought it to Kitty Hawk.

5. The airplane lifted off the ground.
   The airplane flew for 59 seconds.
   The airplane lifted off the ground and flew for 59 seconds.

McGraw-Hill Language Arts
Grade 3, Unit 4, Verbs,
pages 258–259

At Home: Write two sentences about something you would like to invent. Combine the predicates of the sentences. Show your new sentence to a family member.

5

T27

Mechanics and Usage: Apostrophes

RULES

- Use an **apostrophe** (') with nouns or plural nouns to show **possession.**

  The sun's rays   the boys' club

- Add **'s** to **singular nouns** or plural nouns that do not end in **-s.**

  dog's cage   children's smiles

- Add an apostrophe to **plural nouns** ending in **-s.**

  rabbits' noses   cats' whiskers

- Use an apostrophe in a **contraction** to show where letters are missing.

  did not → didn't

  is not → isn't

Underline each word that contains an apostrophe. Write **possession** or **contraction** to show how the apostrophe is used.

1. Shasta's bed is in the corner of my room.

   <u>possession</u>

2. Aren't puppies fun in the morning?

   <u>contraction</u>

3. I can't take her to school with me.

   <u>contraction</u>

4. She plays in our neighbor's yard during the day.

   <u>possession</u>

5. She isn't happy until I get back home.

   <u>contraction</u>

5

McGraw-Hill Language Arts
Grade 3, Unit 4, Verbs,
pages 260–261

At Home: With your family, make a *Do and Don't* list for caring for a family pet. Spell the contraction *don't* correctly each time you use it.

55

Mixed Review

RULES

- **Irregular verbs** have a special spelling for the past tense and when used with *have, has,* or *had.*

  go/went/gone   do/did/done   come/came/come

- Some verbs join with *not* to form contractions. An **apostrophe** (') shows where one or more letters have been left out.

- Use an **apostrophe** with nouns to show **possession.** Add **'s** to singular nouns or plural nouns that do not end in s.

Write the correct past form of each verb in ( ). Add apostrophes where they are missing from other words.

1. My rabbit, Scooter, (run) away once. We couldn't find him.

   ran

2. We (drive) all over the neighborhood looking for him.

   drove

3. My rabbit (do) not come home. Scooters cage was empty.

   did

4. I (begin) to wonder where he might be.

   began

5. Dad (say), "Let's look in the woods."

   said

6. Then a neighbor (give) us information.

   gave

7. He (see) Scooter in a nearby garden. The gardens fence was broken.

   saw

8. Scooter wasnt shy! He (eat) our neighbor's lettuce!

   ate

9. The neighbor (find) him after two days.

   found

10. Scooter never (go) away again.

    went

10

McGraw-Hill Language Arts
Grade 3, Unit 4, Verbs,
pages 262–263

At Home: Ask a family member to tell something that happened to a pet. Listen for the irregular verbs *go, do,* and *come.* Write the forms that you hear.

56

T28

Common Errors with Past-Tense Verbs

RULES
- Add **-ed** to most verbs to show past tense.
- Some verbs have special spellings to show the past tense. It is important to learn which verbs are irregular.
- Some irregular verbs have a different spelling when used with a helping verb.

Verb	Past	With *have, has, or had*
see	saw	seen
come	came	come
bring	brought	brought
eat	ate	eaten
give	gave	given
go	went	gone
say	said	said
begin	began	begun
run	ran	run

Circle the irregular verb in each sentence.

1. Winter has brought a delightful surprise.
2. Snowflakes have begun to fall.
3. We saw icicles in the trees.
4. We brought our sled to the park.
5. We went down the big hill.
6. My family went to our cabin.
7. My uncle came to the cabin, too.
8. Father brought some firewood.
9. Grandmother gave us chestnuts to roast.
10. We ate by the fire.

At Home: Think about some fun things to do in the snow. With your family, write three sentences using irregular verbs to tell about your ideas.

Study Skills: Graphs

RULES
- A **graph** is a diagram that shows the relationship between two or more things. You can use a graph to compare information.
- A **bar graph** uses bars to compare information.
- A **circle graph** compares parts of a whole.
- A **line graph** can show changes over a period of time.

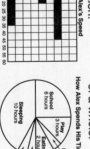
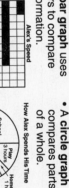

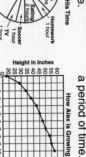

Look at the graphs above. Which graph (bar graph, circle graph, or line graph) would help you answer each question? Write the name of the kind of graph on the line.

1. How does Alex spend his time each day? **circle graph**
2. How tall was Alex at six years old? **line graph**
3. How fast can Alex sing the alphabet? **bar graph**
4. How many inches did Alex grow between the ages of 1 and 3 years old? **line graph**
5. How many hours does Alex spend on homework? **circle graph**
6. How many hours does Alex spend at school? **circle graph**
7. How long does it take Alex to hop ten times? **bar graph**
8. How much time does Alex spend watching television? **circle graph**
9. Does Alex spend more time doing homework or playing? **circle graph**
10. At what age was Alex 50 inches tall? **line graph**

At Home: Ask family members to help you make a graph of how many inches you have grown since you were born.

Vocabulary: Suffixes

- A **suffix** is a word part added to the end of a base word. A **suffix** changes the meaning of a base word.

  sing + er = singer → A singer is a person who sings.

  slow + ly = slowly → To move slowly means to move in a slow way.

  success + ful = successful → To be successful means to be full of success.

I move slowly.

Suffixes	Example	Meaning
-er	_dancer_	one who dances
-or	govern_or_	one who governs
-less	help_less_	without help
-able	fix_able_	able to be fixed
-ly	slow_ly_	in a slow way
-ful	hope_ful_	full of hope

A. Draw lines to match the words on the left with their meanings on the right.

1. understandable — one who talks
2. thankless — full of joy
3. sharply — able to be understood
4. talker — without thanks
5. joyful — in a sharp way

B. Circle the word in each row that has a suffix.

6. (teachable) target telephone
7. polite (photographer) prairie
8. sentence (sunless) sail
9. jealous jungle (faithful)
10. (darkly) dictionary deserve

At Home: Take turns with a family member naming as many jobs as you can that end with the suffix *-er* or *-or*. (Examples: painter, farmer, actor, editor, teacher, firefighter.)

Composition: Writing Descriptions

A **description** can be about persons, places, or things. Descriptive paragraphs have:

- a **main-idea** sentence.
- **sensory details** that describe how things look, taste, smell, sound, and feel.
- an **order that makes sense.**

Read the following descriptive paragraph. Then answer the questions. **Answers may vary.**

In the summer, the Rocky Mountains are a popular place for campers and hikers. These mountains are the perfect place to hike because of the bright blue sky, snowy mountain peaks, and rolling green hills. When hikers climb high above the campsites, the fresh breeze blows gently, and the sweet smell of wildflowers is in the air. It is very quiet except for the wind in the trees and the rushing of small streams over rocks. After spending a day high in the majestic Rocky Mountains, hikers look forward to another visit to this beautiful and peaceful place.

1. Draw a line under the sentence that tells the main idea.

2. What does the main-idea sentence describe?
   the Rocky Mountains

3. Which of your five senses do "very quiet," "wind in the trees," and "rushing of small streams" tell about?
   sound

4. Which words tell you how the mountains look?
   bright blue sky, snowy mountain peaks, rolling green hills

5. Which words describe the sense of smell?
   fresh breeze, sweet smell of wildflowers

At Home: With a family member, think of a beautiful place. Write five sentences describing the place. Use sensory words for all your senses.

Pronouns

RULES

- A **pronoun** is a word that takes the place of one or more nouns.

    Adam works hard. → **He** works hard.

- A pronoun must match the noun or nouns that it replaces.
- To replace a single person, place, or thing, use a **singular pronoun.**

    singular pronouns = I, you, he, she, it, me, him, her

    Liz brought a **violin.** → Liz brought **it.**

- To replace more than one person, place, or thing, use a **plural pronoun.**

    plural pronouns = we, you, they, us, them

    Leroy and Alice are hungry. → **They** are hungry.

Read each sentence. Tell whether the underlined pronoun is singular or plural.

1. Julio watches them play. _____ plural

2. He wants to play basketball, too. _____ singular

3. They do not need any more players on the team. _____ plural

4. Throw the ball to me. _____ singular

5. It goes over the fence. _____ singular

6. He lost the ball. _____ singular

7. Now we can't play basketball. _____ plural

8. I have a baseball. _____ singular

9. All the children now want him to play. _____ singular

10. Julio can play baseball with us. _____ plural

At Home: Scramble the letters of five pronouns. Ask family members to tell what pronouns they are.

Subject Pronouns

RULES

- A **subject pronoun** is used as the subject of a sentence.

    Singular subject pronouns → I, you, he, she, it

    Plural subject pronouns → we, you, they

- A subject pronoun takes the place of the subject of a sentence.

    | Rita | opened the letter. → | She | opened the letter.

    | Kate and Tom | met us. → | They | met us.

Write the subject pronoun of each sentence.

1. They wake up early on Saturday. _____ They

2. She wants to go to the beach. _____ She

3. He wants to go to the swimming pool. _____ He

4. We want to play baseball in the park. _____ We

5. You can go to the beach tomorrow. _____ You

6. I will go to the park with my friends today. _____ I

7. It is too crowded today. _____ It

8. He decides to go to the pool, instead. _____ He

9. They have fun at the pool and at the park. _____ They

10. We all go to the beach the next day. _____ We

At Home: Think of an outdoor activity you enjoy. Use subject pronouns in at least two sentences to tell a family member about the activity.

Object Pronouns

RULES

- An **object pronoun** replaces one or more nouns in the predicate part of a sentence.

- Use an **object pronoun** after an action verb, or after words such as *for, at, of, with, in,* and *to.*

  Singular Object Pronouns → *me, you, him, her, it*

  Plural Object Pronouns → *us, you, them*

  Rina will buy | *the notebooks* | .

  Rina will buy | *them* | .

Write the object pronoun of each sentence.

1. Anna and Justin planned to visit us today.   us

2. We waited for them all afternoon.   them

3. Justin called me at three o'clock.   me

4. He explained what happened to them.   them

5. The tire on Anna's bike had a nail in it.   it

6. Justin knew how to help her.   her

7. They can fix it at the gas station.   it

8. They took the bikes and walked them to the gas station together.   them

9. Justin left a message for you.   you

10. You can meet him at four o'clock.   him

At Home: Ask a family member to tell about visiting a friend. Listen for object pronouns. Make a list of the object pronouns you hear.

Mechanics and Usage:
Using *I* and *Me*

RULES

- Use the pronouns *I* and *me* to write about yourself. Always write the pronoun *I* with a capital letter.

- Use *I* in the subject of a sentence.

  I have work to do.

- Use *me* after an action verb and after words such as *in, into, to, with, by,* or *at.*

  My friends help me.

- When you talk about yourself and another person, name yourself last.

- To help you decide whether to use *I or me*, try the sentence leaving out the other person.

  Ms. Kemper brought pencils for Ellie and me.

  Joel and I arranged the chairs.

Circle the pronoun in ( ) that is correct in each sentence.

1. (I, Me) must read a book about animals.

2. Leroy comes with Kim and (I, me) to the library.

3. Leroy finds a book about snakes for (I, me).

4. (I, Me) do not like snakes.

5. Kim and (I, me) look for another book.

6. Leroy calls (I, me) over to the bookshelf.

7. Now he shows (I, me) some books about dogs.

8. (I, Me) would like to read about dogs.

9. Kim looks at the book with Leroy and (I, me).

10. Leroy, Kim, and (I, me) will all read about dogs.

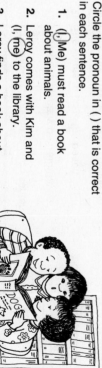

At Home: Ask a family member to tell about a time someone was helpful to him or her. Listen for sentences that use *I* or *me*, and write them down.

Mixed Review

RULES
- A **pronoun** takes the place of one or more nouns.
- A **pronoun** must match the noun it replaces.
- Use a **subject pronoun** as the subject of a sentence.

| Angela | rides every afternoon. |
| **She** | rides every afternoon. |

- Use an **object pronoun** after an action verb or after words such as *for, at, of, with,* and *to.*

Mr. Ramirez leads the horses to | Angela and me |.
Mr. Ramirez leads the horses to | **us** |.

Read each sentence. Circle the word that tells whether the underlined pronoun is a subject pronoun or an object pronoun.

1. Luis invited <u>me</u> to the ranch.   subject   (object)

2. <u>He</u> and Manuel train horses there.   (subject)   object

3. The boys' mother waved to <u>us</u>.   subject   (object)

4. <u>She</u> polishes all of the saddles.   (subject)   object

5. The white horse belongs to <u>her</u>.   subject   (object)

6. Mrs. Ramirez let <u>me</u> ride her horse.   subject   (object)

7. <u>They</u> brought three horses outside.   (subject)   object

8. Luis helped <u>him</u> get on the horse.   subject   (object)

9. <u>He</u> knew exactly what to do.   (subject)   object

10. <u>We</u> rode toward the mountains.   (subject)   object

At Home: With a family member, plan a trip you would like to take. List things your family could do for fun. Write a few sentences about the trip, using *I, we, he, she,* and *they* correctly.

Pronoun-Verb Agreement

RULES
- A **present-tense verb** must agree with its **subject pronoun.**
- Add **-s** to most action verbs in the present tense when you use the pronouns *he, she,* and *it.*

She plays inside.
They play inside.

- Do not add **-s** to an action verb in the present tense when you use the pronouns *I, we, you,* and *they.*

She plays inside.
They play inside.

Circle the action verb in ( ) that is correct in each sentence.

1. It (rain, (rains)) for hours.

2. Kendra (want, (wants)) to play.

3. I ((call), calls) her on the phone.

4. We ((talk), talks) for awhile.

5. "You can ((come), comes) to my house," I tell her.

6. Kendra (ask, (asks)) her mom and dad.

7. They ((say), says) she can come.

8. We ((meet), meets) on the corner of my street.

9. I ((bring), brings) my umbrella.

10. She (wear, (wears)) her raincoat.

At Home: With a family member, draw a picture of something you do with your family. Take turns describing the picture. Use pronoun-verb agreement.

Possessive Pronouns

RULES

- A **possessive pronoun** takes the place of a possessive noun.
  It shows who or what owns something.
  The children's playroom is at the end of the hall.
  Their playroom is at the end of the hall.
- Some possessive pronouns are used before nouns.

my	your	his	her	its	our	your	their

my book   **her** raincoat   **their** project

- Other possessive pronouns can stand alone.

mine	yours	his	hers	its	ours	theirs

These books are **mine.**   Which sandwich is **yours?**

Circle the possessive pronoun in each sentence.

1. (My) little brother Chad was playing in the den.
2. Chad was playing with (his) soccer ball.
3. The ball hit (our) computer by accident.
4. (My) mom was not happy at all.
5. Mom took (his) soccer ball away.
6. (Our) rule is "No soccer in the house."
7. Now I will have to use the computer at (my) school.
8. (Its) screen is bigger than the computer at home.
9. Mom likes (her) keyboard much better, though.
10. Mom and Dad will have (theirs) repaired.

McGraw-Hill Language Arts
Grade 3, Unit 5, Pronouns,
pages 334–335

At Home: Ask family members what uses they have or would have for a computer. Use a possessive pronoun to write their answers.

67

10

McGraw-Hill School Division

Pronoun-Verb Contractions

RULES

- A **contraction** is a shortened form of two words. There are many pronoun-verb contractions.
- Use an **apostrophe** (') to replace the letter or letters that are left out.
  You are late for school. → **You're** late for school.
- Here are some contractions.

he's = he + is or he + has	they're = they + are	he'll = he + will
she's = she + is or she + has	I've = I + have	she'll = she + will
it's = it + is or it + has	you've = you + have	we'll = we + will
I'm = I + am	we've = we + have	you'll = you + will
you're = you + are	they've = they + have	it'll = it + will
we're = we + are		I'll = I + will
		they'll = they + will

Circle the two words that each contraction stands for.

1. they'll   (they will)   they can   they are
2. she's   he will   (she is)   she will
3. you're   you is   they are   (you are)
4. it's   it are   (it is)   it will
5. I'm   (I am)   I will   I is
6. they're   they will   they is   (they are)
7. you've   (you have)   you will   they are
8. he'll   he is   (he will)   it is
9. we're   (we are)   we will   we have
10. you'll   you are   you have   (you will)

McGraw-Hill Language Arts
Grade 3, Unit 5, Pronouns,
pages 336–337

At Home: Make a set of cards with the two parts of a contraction on one side and the contraction on the other. Take turns with a family member looking at the two words and saying the contraction.

68

10

Mechanics and Usage:
Contractions and Possessive Pronouns

RULES
- Be careful not to confuse possessive pronouns with contractions.
- In a **contraction**, an **apostrophe** (') takes the place of the letters that are left out.

  ***They are** going to the zoo.* → ***They're** going to the zoo.*
- **Possessive pronouns** do not have apostrophes.

  *Are they driving in **their** car?*

Circle the contraction or possessive pronoun in each sentence. Write whether it is a possessive pronoun or a contraction.

1. (They're) moving to another city. _____ contraction
2. (Their) house is for sale. _____ possessive pronoun
3. (It's) a big house. _____ contraction
4. We liked to play in (its) big yard. _____ possessive pronoun
5. (Your) family went to see the house. _____ possessive pronoun
6. Do you think (you're) going to buy the house? _____ contraction
7. (It's) great that you will live in that house. _____ contraction
8. (They're) going to get you a big dog now. _____ contraction
9. It will be (their) present to you and your sister. _____ possessive pronoun
10. (Its) size is not important since the yard is big. _____ possessive pronoun

McGraw-Hill Language Arts
Grade 3, Unit 5, Pronouns,
pages 338–339

At Home: Write these sentence starters on index cards: *They're eating _____. He's eating his _____. She's eating her _____.* Take turns completing each card as your family eats a meal together.

 10

69

Mixed Review

RULES
- A **possessive pronoun** shows who or what owns something.

  *Jake and Lil bought this car. It is **their** car.*
- A **contraction** is a shortened form of two words. An **apostrophe** (') replaces the letters that are left out.

  *Tomorrow **they're** driving to the city.*
- Do not confuse possessive pronouns with contractions.

  possessive pronoun → **Its** *engine is quiet.*

  contraction → **It's** *a bright-red car.*

Read each sentence. Write the correct form of the possessive pronoun or the contraction in ( ) on the line.

1. The king asked her to come to (he's, his) castle. _____ his
2. He said, "(I've, Ive) got a special room prepared for you, filled with straw." _____ I've
3. "(I'm, Im) expecting this straw to become gold by tomorrow." _____ I'm
4. "(You'll, Youll) need some help," said a mysterious little man. _____ You'll
5. "In exchange for (your, you're) necklace, I'll spin the straw," he said. _____ your
6. The next day, the king could hardly believe (he's, his) eyes! _____ his
7. (Her, Hers) room was full of gold! _____ Her
8. The little man said, "In return for the gold, you must guess (my, mine) name." _____ my
9. "(Isn't, Isnt) your name Rumpelstiltskin?" she asked. _____ Isn't
10. The mysterious little man snapped (his, he's) fingers and disappeared. _____ his

McGraw-Hill Language Arts
Grade 3, Unit 5, Pronouns,
pages 340–341

At Home: With a family member, make some plans for the weekend. Write about your plans using sentences that begin with the contractions *You'll* and *I'll*.

10

70

Name _____ Date _____

Reteach
71

Common Errors with Pronouns

RULES

Be sure to use the right subject and object pronouns.

- Use a **subject pronoun** as the subject of a sentence.

  This sentence is *not* correct: *Lin and me had a special day yesterday.*

  This sentence is correct: *Lin and I had a special day yesterday.*

- Use an **object pronoun** after an action verb or words such as *for, at, of, with,* and *to.*

  This sentence is *not* correct: *I went to the circus and the zoo with she.*

  This sentence is correct: *I went to the circus and the zoo with **her.***

Read each sentence. Circle the correct pronoun.

1. Lin bought _____ a ticket to the circus.
   (me)   I

2. The trapeze artists flew back and forth above _____ .
   (us)   we

3. _____ watched a man pull pretty white birds out of a hat.
   Him   (I)

4. Then _____ saw clowns climb out of a tiny car.
   them   (we)

5. _____ did lots of funny tricks.
   (They)   Her

6. After lunch _____ went to the zoo.
   (we)   us

7. _____ watched a woman feed a baby tiger with a bottle.
   (I)   Me

8. _____ is a zookeeper.
   (She)   Her

9. The baby tiger looked straight at Lin and _____ .
   I   (me)

10. Then the baby tiger curled up next to _____ and fell asleep.
    she   (her)

10

At Home: With a family member, cut out five pictures from old magazines. Write a sentence about each picture, using pronouns.

71

Name _____ Date _____

Reteach
72

Study Skills: Encyclopedia

RULES

- An **encyclopedia** contains information about people, places, and things.

  Thomas Jefferson   Idaho   bicycles
  Harriet Tubman   Yosemite   frogs

- Each **volume** in an encyclopedia is arranged in alphabetical order according to the letter or letters on its spine. The volumes are numbered to keep them in order.

- The **index** lists the topics in alphabetical order.

- An **encyclopedia on CD-ROM** contains on a computer disk all the information in a set of encyclopedias.

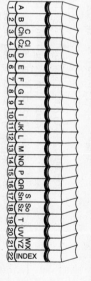

Draw a circle around the correct encyclopedia volume for each topic.

1. robots   13   (16)   9
2. New Zealand   (14)   18   12
3. Cherokee   (3)   5   4
4. beach   6   (2)   9
5. wombat   (21)   12   18

6. England   (6)   5   2
7. glaciers   7   15   (8)
8. kangaroo   (11)   9   14
9. Montana   14   (13)   12
10. aardvark   2   5   (1)

10

At Home: Write the names of several animals. With a family member, use this page to find the encyclopedia volume that has information on each animal.

72

Vocabulary: Homophones

Homophones are words that sound alike but have different spellings and different meanings.

Here are some examples of homophones:

bee, be	A *bee* flew into my room. I hope I won't *be* stung.
nose, knows	Her *nose* is sunburned. She *knows* why it hurts.
eight, ate	There were *eight* apples before Wanda *ate* one of them.

Read aloud the word in the first column. Circle the word in each sentence that sounds the same as this word.

1. ate You can make this breakfast in (eight) minutes.

2. hi Get a mixing bowl down from the (high) shelf.

3. beet (Beat) eggs and milk in the bowl.

4. for Scramble the (four) eggs in a pan.

5. plane Do you like your eggs (plain) or with cheese?

6. sum Cook (some) bacon in another pan.

7. bred Toast a few slices of (bread).

8. poor Who will (pour) the orange juice?

9. eye (I) will get the glasses.

10. two Please can you set the table, (too).

McGraw-Hill Language Arts
Grade 3, Unit 5, Vocabulary,
pages 352–353

At Home: Make an illustrated chart of five homophones. Show your chart to a family member. Explain that these words sound the same but are spelled differently.

☐/10

Composition: Outlining

- An **outline** is a way of organizing ideas you will include in your writing.
- Write the **topic** at the top of the outline.
- List the first **main idea** you plan to include and give it a number. Use a Roman numeral followed by a period.
- Next, list **supporting details** under the main idea. Give each detail a letter.
- Then, list your next main idea and add details as before.
- Ideas written in an outline do not need to be complete sentences. They can be words, phrases, questions, or sentence fragments.

Read the beginning of an outline below. Read the detail sentences. Then draw a line under five detail sentences that belong under the main idea of the outline.

> **Topic: Bluebirds**
> I. What do bluebirds eat?

A. Like to eat insects

B. Build nests in tree holes

C. Will eat berries

D. Fly south in the winter

E. Sometimes eat grapes

F. Will eat beetles

G. Some of them eat caterpillars

At Home: Write the topic "Healthy Foods That Taste Good." Ask a family member to help you list five foods that belong under the main idea.

McGraw-Hill Language Arts
Grade 3, Unit 5, Composition,
pages 354–355

☐/5

Name _____ Date _____

Reteach **75**

Adjectives That Tell *What Kind*

RULES

- An **adjective** is a word that describes a noun.
- Some adjectives tell **what kind** of person, place, or thing the noun is.

*Today is a **special** day.*

tells what kind

The underlined word in each sentence is an adjective. Circle the noun it describes.

1. A large (crowd) waits for the parade.

2. Ben buys a green (balloon).

3. I see colorful (flags).

4. Funny (clowns) make us laugh.

5. The shiny (horns) play a march.

6. We hear the loud (horn).

7. The scouts wear new (uniforms).

8. Brown (horses) prance by.

9. The noisy (crowd) claps and waves.

10. The long (parade) finally ends.

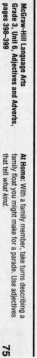

10

McGraw-Hill Language Arts
Grade 3, Unit 6, Adjectives and Adverbs,
pages 398–399

At Home: With a family member, take turns describing a family float you might make for a parade. Use adjectives that tell *what kind*.

75

Name _____ Date _____

Reteach **76**

Adjectives That Tell *How Many*

RULES

- An **adjective** is a word that describes a noun.
- Some adjectives tell **how many**.

***Three** children are good friends.*

tells how many

*They do **many** things together.*

tells how many

Read each sentence. Circle the adjective that describes the underlined noun.

1. (One) day we play inside.

2. Nuna suggests (several) things to do.

3. We choose (one) game to play.

4. The game board has (many) squares.

5. (Several) squares will trap a player.

6. (Few) players miss all the traps.

7. (Many) cards are in a small pile.

8. Nuna draws (one) card.

9. Nuna moves (four) squares.

10. Luis has (two) turns in a row.

11. Mary is behind the other (two) players.

12. Luis lands on (three) traps.

13. Nuna also lands on a (few) traps.

14. We play the game (several) times.

15. Mary wins (three) times.

15

McGraw-Hill Language Arts
Grade 3, Unit 6, Adjectives and Adverbs,
pages 400–401

At Home: Play a game with family members. Then name adjectives that tell how many can play and how long the game takes.

76

McGraw-Hill School Division

T38

Articles

RULES

- **Articles** are special adjectives. The words *a*, *an*, and *the* are articles.
- Use *a* before singular nouns that begin with a consonant.
  ***a* nest**
- Use *an* before singular nouns that begin with a vowel.
  ***an* apple**
- Use *the* before singular nouns and plural nouns.
  ***the* squirrel   *the* squirrels**

Circle the correct article in ( ) to complete each sentence.

1. Do any wild animals live in (the, an) city?

2. You might have (a, an) animal living near you.

3. At night, deer might come from (a, an) park or woods.

4. (The, An) deer might nibble the plants in your garden.

5. (A, An) raccoon might live under a porch.

6. Raccoons will raid (an, the) garbage cans.

7. Squirrels live in (a, an) tree near your house.

8. (A, An) owl might also live in the tree.

9. Mice build nests in (a, the) grass.

10. In the winter, mice may come into (an, the) house.

 10

McGraw-Hill Language Arts
Grade 3, Unit 6, Adjectives and Adverbs,
pages 402–403

At Home: With a family member, make up a story about an owl in a tree and use the articles *a*, *an*, and *the*.

Adjectives That Compare

RULES

- You can use **adjectives** to compare two or more nouns.
- Add *-er* to an adjective to compare two nouns.
  *Today's game was **longer** than last week's game.*
- Add *-est* to compare more than two nouns.
  *Sue is the **greatest** player on our team.*

Write each sentence. Use the correct form of the adjective in ( ).

1. Alice is the (new) team member.
   Alice is the newest team member.

2. Mia is the (fast) runner in our class.
   Mia is the fastest runner in our class.

3. Bet's kick was (longer, longest) than Kevin's.
   Bet's kick was longer than Kevin's.

4. She kicked to her (near) teammate.
   She kicked to her nearest teammate.

5. That player is (quick) than I am.
   That player is quicker than I am.

6. The coach's whistle is (loud) than mine.
   The coach's whistle is louder than mine.

7. The wind is (calm) than it was at noon.
   The wind is calmer than it was at noon.

8. The new field is (smooth) than the old one.
   The new field is smoother than the old one.

9. That team is the (strong) team in town.
   That team is the strongest team in town.

10. Our team's score was the (low) of all.
    Our team's score was the lowest of all.

10

McGraw-Hill Language Arts
Grade 3, Unit 6, Adjectives and Adverbs,
pages 404–405

At Home: Talk about a favorite game with a family member. Use adjectives to compare the action in the game.

Spelling Adjectives That Compare

RULES

Some adjectives change their spelling when -er or -est is added.

- When the adjective ends in a consonant sound and y, change the y to i and add -er or -est.
  shaggy, shaggier, shaggiest
- When the adjective ends in e, drop the e and add -er or -est.
  nice, nicer, nicest
- For adjectives that have a single vowel sound before a final consonant, double the final consonant and add -er or -est.
  big, bigger, biggest

Write the correct spelling of each adjective when the ending is added.

1. happy + er _____ **happier**

2. tan + er _____ **tanner**

3. pale + er _____ **paler**

4. shy + er _____ **shier**

5. gentle + er _____ **genter**

6. furry + est _____ **furriest**

7. noisy + est _____ **noisiest**

8. pretty + est _____ **prettiest**

9. slim + est _____ **slimmest**

10. cute + est _____ **cutest**

10

McGraw-Hill Language Arts
Grade 3, Unit 6, Adjectives and Adverbs,
pages 406–407

At Home: Show the words shaggiest, shiest, and noisiest
to a family member. Take turns making up sentences with
these words.

79

McGraw-Hill School Division

Mechanics and Usage: Using Commas

RULES

- When you read, commas tell you when to pause.
- Use a comma after the name of a person being spoken to.
  Lien, did you have a good time?
- Use a comma after words like yes and no when they begin a sentence.
  Yes, I had a wonderful time.

Add a comma where it belongs in each sentence.

1. Mom, is that the telephone ringing?

2. Yes, can you answer it?

3. No, my hands are sticky.

4. Lien, Pat wants to talk with you.

5. Pat, I was just thinking about you.

6. Lien, can you do something special with us tomorrow?

7. Yes, I would like to do that.

8. Okay, that is great. We are driving to the mountains, and we will hike along Sandy River.

9. Lien, Sandy River is beautiful. Have you ever seen it?

10. No, I have only seen pictures of it.

11. Lien, I hope you can come.

12. Pat, I'll ask my mother.

13. Mom, may I go on a hike and picnic with Pat and her family?

14. Yes, it sounds like a wonderful day.

15. Pat, I will bring my camera, too.

80

McGraw-Hill Language Arts
Grade 3, Unit 6, Adjectives and Adverbs,
pages 408–409

At Home: With a family member, write a conversation
between two friends planning a trip. Use their names at the
beginning of sentences.

15

Mixed Review

RULES

• The article **an** goes before singular nouns that begin with a vowel. The article **a** goes before singular nouns that begin with a consonant.

    *I saw **an** owl in the tree.*
    *Did you ever see **a** duck in a tree?*

• The article **the** goes before singular and plural nouns.
    ***The** ducks don't land in trees.*

• In a sentence in which you speak to someone by name, place a **comma** after the person's name.
    Mrs. Curry, do these ducks live in the pond all year?

• A comma goes after **yes** and **no** when they begin a sentence.
    Yes, they do.

For each sentence, circle the correct article. Write it on the line. Add commas where they belong.

1. Mrs. Curry, are you going to feed _____ ducks at the pond?   (the)   a

2. Yes, I have _____ loaf of bread for them.   (a)   an

3. Fred, do you want _____ piece of bread?   (a)   an

4. No, I brought _____ orange.   a   (an)

5. Ducks don't like _____ taste of oranges.   a   (the)

6. Laura, please don't splash _____ water.   (the)   an

7. That duck has _____ long beak.   (a)   (a)

8. Mrs. Curry, may I give it _____ piece of bread?   (a)   the

9. Yes, here is _____ crust.   an   (the)

10. Wow, what _____ hungry duck that is!   a   (a)

McGraw-Hill Language Arts
Grade 3, Unit 6, Adjectives and Adverbs,
pages 410–411

 10

At Home: Play a game of "I Spy" with a family member. Take turns writing sentences that begin with "I spy (a, an, the) . . ." Use the correct article before each noun.

Adverbs

RULES

• An **adverb** is a word that tells more about a verb.
• Adverbs tell **how, when,** and **where** an action takes place.

    *The train moves **swiftly**.* → how
    *Grandma arrives **tomorrow**.* → when
    *I see the train **there**.* → where

Circle the adverb that tells about the underlined verb.

1. Dylan's grandmother <u>arrives</u> (today).

2. Her train will <u>come</u> (soon).

3. Dad <u>parks</u> the car (nearby).

4. They <u>go</u> (inside).

5. A woman (kindly) <u>answers</u> their questions.

6. Dylan <u>looks</u> (around).

7. Many travelers <u>sit</u> (quietly).

8. Some people <u>wait</u> (anxiously).

9. Dad and Dylan <u>walk</u> (outside).

10. Dylan <u>looks</u> (down).

11. Dad <u>listens</u> (carefully).

12. The train will <u>arrive</u> (early).

13. The train (slowly) <u>stops</u>.

14. Dylan <u>sees</u> Grandma (ahead).

15. He (eagerly) <u>waves</u> to her.

McGraw-Hill Language Arts
Grade 3, Unit 6, Adjectives and Adverbs,
pages 412–413

15

At Home: With family members, act out meeting someone at a train station. What adverbs describe how you act?

Adverbs That Tell *How*

RULES
- Some **adverbs** tell *how* an action takes place.
- Adverbs that tell **how** usually end in *-ly*.

The sun shone **bright** *ly* .   The wind blows **gent** *ly* .

Circle the adverb that describes the underlined verb. Then, write it on the line.

1. The woods quietly wait for us. _____ quietly

2. Deena and I eagerly enter the woods. _____ eagerly

3. Someone clearly marked a path. _____ clearly

4. We easily follow the path. _____ easily

5. We explore curiously. _____ curiously

6. Birds sing sweetly. _____ sweetly

7. The brook flows smoothly. _____ smoothly

8. Suddenly a bird flies. _____ Suddenly

9. Its wings flap loudly. _____ loudly

10. Deena anxiously looks at me. _____ anxiously

11. Deena grabs my hand tightly. _____ tightly

12. She quickly becomes frightened. _____ quickly

13. I whisper softly to her. _____ softly

14. I calmly explain what it was. _____ calmly

15. We happily go home. _____ happily

15

McGraw-Hill Language Arts
Grade 3, Unit 6, Adjectives and Adverbs,
pages 414–415

At Home: Listen to sounds around you with a family member. Use adverbs to describe the sounds you hear.

83

McGraw-Hill School Division

Adverbs That Tell *When* or *Where*

RULES
- Some **adverbs** tell **when** or **where** an action takes place.

We wake up **early** .   We drive **far** .
→ tells when   → tells where

Here are some adverbs that tell **when** and **where**.

When		Where	
always	next	ahead	here
early	soon	around	outside
first	then	away	there
later	today	far	up

Write **when** or **where** on the line to show what each underlined adverb tells.

1. Today, we go to the beach. _____ when

2. We go there every year. _____ where

3. We leave home early. _____ when

4. First, we travel for an hour. _____ when

5. We always eat a picnic breakfast. _____ when

6. We stop here to eat. _____ where

7. Then, we drive again. _____ when

8. I turn to the car window and look out. _____ where

9. Ned looks around, too. _____ where

10. Soon, Ned sees the ocean! _____ when

11. Ned rushes to the water first. _____ when

12. Mom and I join him there. _____ where

13. Later, we walk down the beach. _____ when

14. We see shells everywhere. _____ where

15. It is wonderful here. _____ where

McGraw-Hill Language Arts
Grade 3, Unit 6, Adjectives and Adverbs,
pages 416–417

At Home: Where does your family like to go together? Take turns writing about one favorite place. Use adverbs that tell *when* and *where*.

15

84

T42

Combining Sentences: Adjectives and Adverbs

RULES

- Two sentences that tell about the same person, place, or thing can be **combined by adding an adjective** from one sentence to the other sentence.

  I'm going to a party. → *I'm going to a surprise party.*
  It is a surprise.

- Two sentences that tell about the same action can be **combined by adding an adverb** from one sentence to the other sentence.

  The party is tomorrow. → *I'm going to a party tomorrow.*
  I'm going to a party.

Combine each pair of sentences. Add an adjective or adverb to one of the sentences. Write the new sentence. The first part of each combined sentence is written for you.

1. I wrapped a present. I wrapped it yesterday.

   I wrapped _a present yesterday._

2. The kitten found my present. My present was colorful.

   The kitten _found my colorful present._

3. She tore the wrapping paper. The wrapping paper was pretty.

   She tore _the pretty wrapping paper._

4. I found a paper bag. The paper bag was big.

   I found _a big paper bag._

5. I hid the present in the bag. I hid the present today.

   I hid _the present in the bag today._

McGraw-Hill Language Arts
Grade 3, Unit 6, Adjectives and Adverbs,
pages 418–419

At Home: Show a family member the picture of the kitten tearing the wrapping paper. Write two sentences about the kitten. Use adjectives or adverbs to combine the sentences.

Mechanics and Usage: Quotation Marks

RULES

- Use **quotation marks (" ")** to show that someone is speaking.
- Quotation marks come at the beginning and end of a person's exact words.

  "Where are you, Don?" Andrea called.
  "It's time to leave," she said.

The underlined words in each sentence show the words someone says. Write out the sentences with the quotation marks added in the correct place.

1. Hurry up, Andrea said to Don.

   "Hurry up," Andrea said to Don.

2. I'm coming, Don answered.

   "I'm coming," Don answered.

3. But I can't find my bus pass, he added.

   "But I can't find my bus pass," he added.

4. Andrea said, I will help you look for it.

   Andrea said, "I will help you look for it."

5. I've looked everywhere, Don replied.

   "I've looked everywhere," Don replied.

6. When did you last see it? Andrea asked.

   "When did you last see it?" Andrea asked.

7. Don explained, I used it yesterday.

   Don explained, "I used it yesterday."

8. Look in your jacket pocket, Andrea said.

   "Look in your jacket pocket," Andrea said.

9. It's there! Don shouted.

   "It's there!" Don shouted.

10. He said, I looked everywhere but my pocket.

    He said, "I looked everywhere but my pocket."

McGraw-Hill Language Arts
Grade 3, Unit 6, Adjectives and Adverbs,
pages 420–421

At Home: Listen to two family members talking. Write down what they say. Show your family how to add quotation marks where they belong.

Mixed Review

RULES

- An **adverb** tells more about a verb.
- Adverbs that tell **how** often end with **-ly**.

  *Dad woke up **suddenly**.* (sudden + -ly)

- Some adverbs tell **where** or **when** an action takes place.

  *He stood and looked **around**.* (where)

  ***Then** he walked into the hallway.* (when)

Draw a line under each verb. Then use an adverb from the box to complete each sentence. **Answers may vary. Possible answers are given.**

swiftly	soon	loudly	eagerly
nearby	peacefully	rapidly	outside
immediately	quickly		

1. Dad listened <u>eagerly</u> for the sound.

2. <u>Soon</u> I awoke, too.

3. Heavy footsteps approached <u>rapidly</u>.

4. They tapped <u>loudly</u> across the porch.

5. Dad lit the porch light <u>immediately</u>.

6. We both looked <u>outside</u>.

7. Dad <u>swiftly</u> opened the door.

8. Something ran <u>quickly</u> off the porch.

9. We saw the neighbor's dog Thunder <u>nearby</u>.

10. We slept <u>peacefully</u> the rest of the night.

10

At Home: Play What Sound Is It? One person makes a sound in another room and the other person guesses what it is. Use adverbs to help describe the sound.

87

Common Errors with Adjectives

RULES

Follow these rules when comparing **two** nouns:

- When the adjective is short, like *green*, add **-er**.

  *Mr. Chang's lawn is **greener** than our lawn.*

- When the adjective is long, like *comfortable*, use *more* with the adjective.

  *This chair is **more comfortable** than that chair.*

Follow these rules when comparing **more than two**:

- When the adjective is short, like *kind*, add **-est**.

  *Mrs. Thomas is the **kindest** person I know.*

- When the adjective is long, like *interesting*, use **most** with the adjective.

  *This book is the **most interesting** book I've read.*

Read each sentence. Circle each adjective that compares.

1. Today is the (hottest) day of the year.

2. The temperature is (higher) than yesterday.

3. The temperature seems (cooler) at the beach than at our house.

4. The waves are (bigger) than before.

5. Near the ocean is the (most comfortable) place to be.

6. The sand looks (darker) near the water.

7. Your sand castle is (more beautiful) than mine!

8. This beach is the (nicest) one I've seen.

9. The air is (fresher) here than at home.

10. This has been the (most relaxing) day ever!

10

At Home: Ask your family to help you write three sentences describing the weather, using adjectives that compare.

88

Page 89

Study Skills: Thesaurus

RULES

- **Synonyms** are words that have the same or almost the same meaning.

  Happy means almost the same as *glad*.
  Hard means almost the same as *difficult*.

- **Antonyms** are words that have opposite meanings.

  Happy means the opposite of *sad*.
  Hard means the opposite of *easy*.

- A **thesaurus** is a book of synonyms and antonyms. It is a place to find the exact word you need to make your meaning clear.

Look at the first word in each row. Circle the synonym for that word in the row. Then find the antonym in the row. Write it on the line.

1. **large** (big) tiny middle far
   tiny _____

2. **bright** sweet dull beautiful (shiny)
   dull _____

3. **neat** (tidy) inquire messy new
   messy _____

4. **scared** brave calm (afraid) angry
   brave _____

5. **fast** (quick) far slow late
   slow _____

McGraw-Hill Language Arts
Grade 3, Unit 6, Study Skills,
pages 432–433

At Home: Play a synonym/antonym game. Make 20 word cards. Take turns drawing a card. Write a synonym or antonym on it. The first one to complete 10 cards wins.

Page 90

Vocabulary: Synonyms and Antonyms

- **Synonyms** are words that have the same or almost the same meaning.

  near / close   *big / large*   *begin / start*

- **Antonyms** are words that have opposite meanings.

  up / down   *hot / cold*   *high / low*

A. Choose a synonym from the box to replace each underlined word. Write the word on the line.

| silky | bend | huge |
| beautiful | strolls |

1. My dog is a handsome animal. _____
   beautiful

2. His large brown eyes are friendly. _____
   huge

3. He has a smooth coat. _____
   silky

4. We like to go for walks. _____
   strolls

5. People lean over to pet my dog. _____
   bend

B. Choose an antonym from the box to replace each underlined word. Write the word on the line.

| sits | warm | quiet |
| close | thick |

6. My cat is a noisy creature. _____
   quiet

7. She stands in my lap for hours. _____
   sits

8. Her thin fur feels soft and silky. _____
   thick

9. When I stroke her head, her eyes open happily. _____
   close

10. My cat is a cold friend. _____
    warm

McGraw-Hill Language Arts
Grade 3, Unit 6, Vocabulary,
pages 434–435

At Home: Play a Synonym/Antonym game with family members. Write down a list of words. Say each one aloud and let family members call out a synonym or antonym for it.

Composition: Beginning, Middle, End

All good stories have three parts:

- The **beginning** tells who and what the story is about and where and when it takes place.
- The **middle** tells the events, actions, and problems in a story.
- The **end** tells how the story comes out in a way that makes sense.

The beginning tells who or what we will read about. → Johnny Appleseed spent his life going around the country planting apple trees.

The middle tells what happens. → He got the seeds from cider mills. Johnny Appleseed gave the seeds to settlers. He wanted everyone to have apples.

The ending lets us know the story is finished. → We can thank Johnny Appleseed for many of our apple trees.

Circle **beginning** or **end** to tell where each pair of sentences would go in a story.

1. Stormy was the fastest horse in the county. (beginning) end

2. And that's what happened to a horse named Stormy. beginning (end)

3. The girl turned out to be the best trumpet teacher in the state of Texas! beginning (end)

4. Once there was a girl who wanted to play the trumpet. (beginning) end

5. No one ever heard from Sailor Sam again. beginning (end)

6. Have you heard the story of Sailor Sam? (beginning) end

7. Long ago, there was a little house in the big city. (beginning) end

8. The little house was never lonely again. beginning (end)

9. Years later, we published the book and sold 100 copies! beginning (end)

10. One day, Dad and I wrote a book about fishing. (beginning) end

McGraw-Hill Language Arts
Grade 3, Unit 6, Composition,
pages 436–437

At Home: Read a favorite story with your family. Find the beginning, middle, and end of the story. Can you think of another end for the story?

10

91